Shakedown:
The Fleecing of the Garden State

for The people!!!

Shakedown

The Fleecing of the Garden State

By Carl J. Mayer

Essential Books
Washington, D.C.

Cover Art by Warren Linn. Cover Design by Elizabeth C. Schramm.

Thanks to the following news organizations for permission to reprint articles or excerpts of articles contained herein: The New YorkTimes. Copyright 1998 by the New York Times. Reprinted by permission. CBS News Sixty Minutes. Newsday. The Times, Trenton, N.J. All Rights Reserved. Reprinted with permission. The Princeton Packet.Asbury Park Press. Newark Star-Ledger. The Courier News. Home News and Tribune. American Fitness. The Denver Post. Trentonian. Town Topics.

ISBN 0-9621259-8-9

Library of Congress Cataloging in Publication Data Available.

Essential Books
P.O. Box 19405
Washington, D.C. 20036

To the memory of my grandfathers, Frank and Arnold,
who taught me about public service;

To my grandmothers, Frances and Ida,
who teach me about people;

To my father Arno,
who teaches me about ideas and industry;

To my mother, Nancy,
who teaches me about friends and charity;

To my brother Daniel,
who teaches me about education and family;

To my sister-in-law Sarah,
who teaches me about diplomacy;

To my nephew Samuel and my niece Ruby,
who teach me about the importance of the future.

ACKNOWLEDGEMENTS

I want to record my deep gratitude to Ralph Nader, a principled and courageous leader in a nation that urgently needs people of his vision. Thanks also to John Richard, America's leading behind-the-scenes activist who makes things happen, and to Gene Stilp, a creative thinker who inspires others. Special thanks to Bruce Afran, a lawyer who fights the tough cases and wins.

I am indebted to many friends, neighbors and activists who are always willing to debate ideas and share a common interest in advancing social justice: William Taylor, Eliot Spitzer, Silda Wall, Jerome Marcus, Caroline Hall, Mary Penney, Scott and Lisa Cromar, George Plimpton, Remar Sutton, Robert Hosford, Jonathan Dushoff, Jonathan Earle, Daphne and Arnold Lazarus, Lewis Black, Scott Blakeman, Earl and June Adler, Peter and Cheryl Engel, Marge Engel, Anne Beaumont, Julia Bernheim, Sharon and Alan Bilanin, Jason Bilanin, Mary Bonotto, Sandra and Jonathan Brown, Dan Brown, Jimmy Tarlau, Don Dileo, Walter and Ruth Burger, Jackie Burger, Frank Glaser, Michelle Burger, Tom Cramer, Susie Burger, David Wagner, Jerry Barbanel, David Felsenthal, Jason Brown, Ellen Livingston, Richard Grossman, Sally Frank, Lorenzo Canizeras, Mary Cozzolino, Barry and Sandy Silber, Gayle Herschkopf, Jonathan and Jenny Crumiller, David Eden, Earl Gray, Steve Welzer, Madelyn Hoffman, Nick Mellis, Delores Phillips, Rachel Storch, Naomi Wolfensohn, Ellen

Feinsot, Gary Ferdman, Vicky Fox, Alan Freid, Naomi Friedman, Elaine and Philip Germaine, Robert and Ellen Ginsberg, Josh Handler, Joe Mosley, Stuart Hutchinson, Elena Kagan, Jonah Kaplan, Karen Cotton, Billie and Christopher King, Patricia Klensh-Balmer, Roger Martindell, Cyrus Mehri, Myra Monteleone, George and Lenore Abrams, Ted Frankel, Gail Munro, Sara Wolfensohn, Tom Nussbaumer, Mary Penney, Maxine Moore, Carl and Elizabeth Schorske, Sheldon Wolin, Matthew Rothschild, Bradley Siciliano, Larry Hamm, Joe Fortunato, Art Rosen, Jim Mohn, Gary Novocelski, Louis Riley, Micah Sifry, Katrina vanden Heuvel, Monica Stockman, Beverly Kidder, Harriet Sunshine, Christine Stoll, Pat S., Bob C., Linda and Kathy, Allen Nairn, Norman and Ann Weinstein, Robin Williams, Lisabeth and Norman Winarsky, Ed Bray, John Sicino, John Dermody, E.J. "Red" Johnson, Robert Becker, David Eichenbaum, Celinda Lake, Jennifer Sosin, Rich Schlackman, Robert Becker, Steve and Karin Slaby, Henriette Mantel, Emily Cook, Robert Delgato, Steve and Karin Slaby, Russell Mokhiber, Elaine Gilbert, David Dixon, Wanda Alston, Stacy Ho, Larry Schwartz, John Luke, Monroe Freedman, David Yellin, Scott Goodstein, Peter Levy, Antoine Bernheim, Naomi Goldberg, Chloe Mantel and Patricia Ireland.

I am most grateful to an ace editorial team: Alan Hirsch, Stephanie Donne, Donna Colvin and Robert Weissman.

Table of Contents

CHAPTER ONE

HOW I MET MISS ATLANTIC CITY
AND HEAR-SAY THE GENIE

[M]ake not my Father's house an house of merchandise."
— St. John, ch.2, ver. 16.

What, you might ask, is a nice young man doing with Miss Atlantic City (in a tiara and red-sequin dress) draped on one arm and "Hear-Say The Genie" (a 6'6" African-American transvestite on stilts wearing a purple and gold lame turban, an open-chest purple shirt with gold chains and billowing purple pants) on the other?

I was undercover, exploring how politics works in this country. "Sixty Minutes" had asked me to accompany one of their producers with a hidden camera to Atlantic City and Washington D.C. to help expose the influence of money on politics in America.

Miss Atlantic City and "Hear-Say the Genie" were stationed at an exhibit in Washington D.C. put on by the Atlantic City Chamber of Commerce. I was posing with the two at a swank Washington hotel; tourists in the lobby clicked away with their cameras as one of the big political events of the season unfolded. The Chamber of Commerce busily plied anyone they could with drinks, trinkets, and a general good time.

Miss Atlantic City looked forward to competing in the Miss America contest someday; "Hear-Say," employed at the Trump Taj Mahal casino, was on loan to the Chamber of Commerce. (He gave me his business card; he appears at private parties). It was February, 1996.

Unknown to the wildly attired duo, while I posed

with them, a "Sixty Minutes" cameraman rolled film. The camera was hidden on his body. (I promised not to tell where it was. I can reveal only that the miniature technology was originally developed by the Israeli secret service, the Mossad, to spy on the Syrians.)

I had agreed to work with "Sixty Minutes" after the news program approached me in the summer of 1995. Correspondent Morley Safer had read an opinion piece I authored in the *New York Times*. Apparently he was amused, and thought it would make a humorous show illuminating the problems of our democracy:

The Importance of Being Anyone at All
By Carl J. Mayer
PRINCETON, N.J. — The next time you write a check for state or local taxes, you might ponder how much of your money will be spent to support the gambling and drinking activities of the people you elect to serve you. At a time of tightening state and local budgets across the country, the taxpayer-financed junket remains one of the few expenses no one touches.

My experience as a neophyte elected official illustrates the phenomenon. As a new town committeeman, I was informed that my first official appearance would be at the annual New Jersey State League of Municipalities convention for elected officials in Atlantic City.

Convening in Atlantic City to study municipal governance is like assembling a religious retreat in Times Square on the problem of virtue. So what if four out of the last seven mayors of Atlantic City were convicted of crimes? The crucial point is that there are scads of casinos, and virtually every local elected official in New Jersey can be entertained in chandeliered ballrooms by corporate representatives. The townships pick up the tab for the hotel rooms and most of the meals (I reimbursed the citizens of Princeton, the township that elected me).

The Princeton delegation was booked at the Trump Plaza. With no clocks, few phones and no place to sit, a casino is not exactly a conducive setting for sober discussion of public policy issues. The atmosphere was favorable, however, for one of the convention's main purposes: enabling corporations to pitch products and services to local officials who need to purchase, with tax dollars, everything from software to insurance to pavement markings.

The assembled delegates, overwhelmingly male, were plied with liquor, food and gifts by — in what must have been a coincidence — attractive women representing hundreds of companies, including Fortune 500 enterprises like Bell Atlantic, General Motors and Chemical Bank.

My complimentary Midlantic Bank Post-It notes and Charmin samples deepened my understanding of the political process. Lobbyists competed ferociously to stage the most sumptuous reception for junketeers. The clear winner was K. Hovnanian Enterprises, one of the largest real-estate developers in New Jersey. Hundreds of politicos thronged around their regal display of oysters, shrimp, prime rib and ice sculptures. (Hovnanian is scheduled to build a housing development in Princeton, joining recently opened Wal-Mart and Home Depot outlets. Thus our downtown shopping district can take its place on the endangered species list along with so many others.)

Corporate leaders understand that cultivating local politicians can boost the bottom line, and that the laws controlling contracts are often looser at the local and state level — even though hundreds of millions of taxpayer dollars are at stake. A casino is an apt metaphor for the spending of municipal money: decisions about local purchasing can be influenced at gaudy promotional booths rather than through a sober competitive bidding process.

The largess doesn't end at the state line, either. And sometimes the junkets are corporate-sponsored. The New Jersey Chamber of Commerce has for years chartered an Amtrak train to transport more than 1,000 politicians, businesspeople and lobbyists from New Jersey to Washington for its annual Congressional reception, a junket known in the local press as the "pub crawl on wheels" and the "pork-barrel express." The ride, whose expense is partly reimbursed by the lobbyists, gives the select crowd a few hours of extra special access.

This event became so popular that three years ago the Chamber of Commerce inaugurated a second train to transport state legislative leaders to, of course, Atlantic City. No thought is ever given to bringing convention dollars to impoverished New Jersey cities like Trenton, Newark or Camden.

The amount spent on local and state junkets nationwide is impossible to estimate, because reporting requirements are much less stringent than at the Federal level. Some states are more vigilant than others. Wisconsin has a law dating back to 1957 banning any gifts — even a cup of coffee — to state legislators. Iowa, Minnesota, South Carolina and Kentucky also have tough laws. Even Wisconsin, though, allows taxpayers to pick up the tab for lawmakers who attend events partially sponsored by corporations.

And most states, including New Jersey, lack all but the most minimal restrictions on corporate-sponsored and taxpayer-financed junkets. As the momentum grows for "real reform" in government, banning this kind of influence-peddling at the local and state level would be a good start.

By the way, I just received my invitation for this year's Atlantic City convention in November.

Two days after the article appeared in the *New York Times*, I received a phone call from a "Sixty Minutes" producer. She said that Morley Safer asked her to set up a meeting with me. In discussions at a diner, the producers asked whether I would be amenable to attending some New Jersey functions with a hidden cameraman. Although reluctant, I decided that casting light on the lobbying process could help reform the system. In the words of former Supreme Court Justice Felix Frankfurter: "Sunlight is the best disinfectant."

The first event we attended was the New Jersey League of Municipalities Convention in Atlantic City. (The League represents New Jersey's 566 municipalities.) At the convention I met the undercover cameraman who followed me around from booth to booth; he filmed all the bizarre promotional gimmicks put on by the lobbyists: free-throw contests, roulette wheels, treasure hunts, carnival wheels operated by scantily clad women, etc.

Ostensibly, the event exists to provide seminars for elected officials. There were as many people in the casinos as at the seminars, and some of the sessions were utterly bizarre. Consider one meeting entitled: "Hazardous Waste and New Jersey: Perfect Together?" The seminar described a New Jersey program which offered New Jersey towns millions of dollars to have a hazardous waste site built in their township. Imagine taxpayers subsidizing a program that benefits the nuclear industry and poisons citizens.

(At one point I approached the CEO of a leading nuclear utility in New Jersey and asked whether he might consider offering my hometown of Princeton a few million to take the radioactive waste. His response: "Oh, we would never consider approaching Princeton. The citizens there are too smart and educated to go for something like that." Translation: poor, uneducated and disadvantaged communities beware.)

After a day of filming, CBS had a second crew with a camera in plain view enter the cavernous Atlantic City convention hall and interview some lobbyists. One lobbyist offered a cash bribe to the cameraman to stop filming his company's exhibition booth; the producer observed that in all his years with "Sixty Minutes", this was the first time he had ever been offered a bribe.

Our next project was to take the Chamber of Commerce train to Washington. For this, "Sixty Minutes" hired a helicopter to film the train, and brought a second hidden camera on board the train; a third live camera met us at the other end. With a helicopter buzzing the train and a hidden camera on board, this was the closest thing to a James Bond experience I ever had.

Before the train even left New Jersey for Washington, the bar cars were seven deep and the passengers very happy. I was offered by various business lobbyists the following special favors: an opportunity to visit the NFL film archives in Canton Ohio (apparently only NFL players have access to the archives, but the Chamber of Commerce has arranged for a special day of viewing highlight films, including Super Bowl footage, unavailable to the public); a Caribbean cruise; a golf tour of the Bahamas; a free day at the racetrack, and several other junkets I do not remember.

Lobbyists for many Fortune 500 corporations were on the train: Coke, ATT, General Motors, Chemical Bank and a host of others. One lobbyist, working for a Fortune 500 company, explained to me how easy it is to get a special bill for just one corporation passed through the legislature: Simply hold out the prospect of jobs and the legislature will grant all the tax relief and subsidies any company could ask for.

The "Sixty Minutes" episode aired on May 12,

1996:

Mike Wallace: *His name is Carl Mayer and in the pecking order of American political office he is just about as small time as you can get. A very little fish. A committeeman for the Township of New Jersey. But in the world of political lobbying there is no such thing as a little fish. Now then, lobbying can be a legal effort to influence politicians. Some say it is not influence but buying politicians that is involved. And it is not just a big time Washington phenomena, as Carl Mayer learned just days after he was elected. Morley Safer reports that the lobbying begins at the very beginning.*

Carl Mayer: *Lobbying and giving money to politicians is the best return on an investment in the entire free world.*

Morley Safer: *And it starts in little places like Princeton, New Jersey.*

Carl Mayer: *The corporate money interest tentacles extend even to the smallest shire and borough in the nation.*

MS: *When Mayer was elected he met the full force of those tentacles. In response he wrote a piece about it in the New York Times, called, "The Importance of Being Anyone At All."*

CM: *Approximately a week or ten days after being elected, there was this junket down in Atlantic City at the Casinos where the corporations sponsored the event and it was almost my initial coming out — as it were — as a politician.*

(In Atlantic City — pictures of convention and corporate booth with enormous Wheel of Fortune.)

Unidentified Man: *We'll spin the wheel. We'll see if you come up as a winner.*

MS: *A coming out party organized every year by the New Jersey League of Municipalities where every level of local government convenes in theory to exchange ideas for better government.*

(Footage of signboards at convention showing Fortune 500 sponsors like New York Life, The Travelers, and Bell Atlantic)

But also invited is every level of corporate America trying to sell stuff or to just meet the men and women whose votes will decide what to buy and where to spend it. From $25,000 police cars to $25 gadgets that pick up trash.

CM: *The entire convention really centers around attempting to extract favors from government. One big party, junket, fiesta, hootenanny...*

MS: *When you went to Atlantic City this year we went with you on the quiet. You were in cahoots with us? Right? It meant using a hidden camera so we could view the political education of Carl Mayer in the purest possible way. So off we went, to the same hall that Miss America is crowned. What's at stake is New Jersey's $7 billion dollar municipal pie. Mayer may be a part-time committeeman making a measly $5,500 per year, but his township board has a $20 million dollar budget to spend.*

CM: *The primary purpose of this is for the lobbyists to get their hands on the elected leaders and in particular to get their hands on the billions of dollars that municipalities and the state spends every year on the various products.*

MS: *A turkey shoot for anyone trying to sell anything to every town.*

(Footage of a fish tank at a Mobil Oil exhibit)

CM: *Are you saying if you spill Mobil Oil, the fish can eat it?*

Mobil Oil Exhibitor: *Bingo.*

MS: *Every booth has a pretty girl or a goofy gimmick.*

CM: *Do I think they are buying politicians with a 2 cent ruler or a ball - no. But do I think that, that combined with the receptions, and the campaign contributions and the lobbyists, skews the system in favor of the big money corporate contributors - absolutely.*

MS: *Whatever it does, it gives them the kind of access to you that they might not otherwise have.*

CM: *That's right.*

MS: *And at the taxpayer's expense. Most municipalities pay for their officials to attend while corporations and lobbyists write their costs off as business expenses. And what does the taxpayer get back?*

Scene Change to **William Dressel:** *The taxpayer is getting more informed local officials by going to the conference, by attending the session.*

MS: *William Dressel is the Executive Director of the League of Municipalities.*

William Dressel: *You can give me two or three officials that say it is fun and games, I can give you 50 or 60 municipal officials without any problem at all who will say that it is an educational experience and that they have learned more from going to our conference and participating in the sessions than any other forum provided them.*

Back to **CM:** *Well, if that is education then I would like to see what happens when corporate lobbyists really party? Sure there are seminars. But most people aren't in the seminars. They are in the gaming rooms in the casinos or they're down on the floor with the corporate exhibitors.*

(Picture of treasure chests, games and prizes)

MS: *It is more a sales convention than the tedious business of governing. A TV set or a boom box may not make a politician a friend for life but you've got to start somewhere. One firm had a treasure chest. A reminder perhaps that so much in life is dumb luck. An environmental cleanup company staged a free-throw shooting contest open only to officials who control the municipal budget.*

(Picture of elected officials shooting baskets for cash prizes)

MS: *When Executive Director Dressel saw all of this he* *said we weren't presenting the full story.*

Scene changed to **Dressel:** *The camera lies here. The camera shows only three or four instances of what is happening on an exhibit floor. It is not showing all of the other exhibits, showing the effect of all the exhibits, it is not showing the information that is also being disseminated at this booth. It is not showing anything else.*

Back to **MS:** *So far nothing dishonest has happened. Correct? Nobody said, "Hey Carl, here is a couple of hundred bucks." Do you know if it has ever happened?*

CM: *Do I know if anyone has said, "Hey Carl..." Other than the incident with the camera crew...*

MS: *That's a hundred dollars discretely folded inside a business card that was given to our cameraman who was filming in plain view at a booth operated by the United Gunite Construction Company, a cement products manufacturer. New Jersey uses a lot of cement. The cash was returned a few minutes later.*

Scene changed to **United Gunite Representative:** *I was going to buy you lunch.*

60 Minutes Camera-man, Off camera: *No I can't. They would fire my butt.*

UGR: *If I buy your lunch?*

Back to **MS:** *Who says there is no such thing as a free lunch? But what was it really for? We couldn't figure it out,* *and neither could the Executive Director of the affair.*

Dressel: *What was it for? He just wanted to give it out. Pass out money to people just walking by? That's totally, totally, totally .... inappropriate behavior.*

MS: *Especially inappropriate given that the Atlantic City event is something like a blind date. Just foreplay to the main event three months later where the politicians literally get taken for a ride. It is know as the "gravy train."*

(Shots of lobbyists mobbing the bar car)

MS: *Once a year the New Jersey Chamber of Commerce rents an 18 car train. This year we asked Carl Mayer to get on board with our hidden camera where he could mingle and schmooze with almost 2,000 politicians, lobbyists, and business people who pay $450 for this simple pleasure. The lobbyists and business people want contracts and favors. The politicians want campaign contributions. The theme here is really getting to know you as the train snakes and drinks its way from Newark to Washington, DC, ending with a gala dinner with the state's congressional delegation. Lobbyist on train: The fun of this thing is to walk all 18 cars. Because there are parties in other cars ... the CIT corporations...New Jersey Bell.*

Scene changed to **Joan Verplank, NJ Chamber of Commerce President:** *I think we need to be cozy with the legislature. It is so social, it is so crowded, so diverse. I don't know how you would really deliver a political agenda.*

MS: *Because nobody's sober.*

Verplank: *No, that's not true, it's really not true. I think the days of people having too much to drink ended about five years ago, quite honestly.*

People on train: *Most of it is networking.*

CM: *Everybody uses the word networking, lobbying or something else not quite so polite.*

MS: *Of course, in an election year there is one underlying reason why so many politicians and their campaign go along for the ride.*

People on train: *Money, money, money.*

CM: *You've heard the phrase: 'Money is the Mother's Milk of politics.' I really think that money is the crack cocaine of American politics. They start you out at the local level, you get nickel bags, little gifts, little junkets and then there is a little more when you get to the state level. You are off to the big-time campaign contributions ... by the time you get to Washington.*

(Scene Changed to Morley Safer interviewing Chamber of Commerce Chair Verplank in her office)

MS: *One of the things that happen on these trains is those politicians are approached by the Chamber of Commerce or the local Chamber of Commerce or businesses and they are invited on golf outings and Caribbean Cruises.*

Verplank: *Who in the world told you that? I've never heard anything like that. In all honesty, I have never* *heard anything like that.*

(Scene change to hidden camera on Train)

Lobbyist: *We have a Golf tournament in Tavistock.*

CM: *When is that?*

Lobbyist: *May 6th. I'm doing a Chamber cruise. That's a fun one...We're going to the Eastern Caribbean in August...You want to go?*

Scene Change to **CM:** *The junkets are the tip of the iceberg. Then you have the lobbyists they hire, then the gifts, then the golf outings, then the campaign contributions, then the campaign contributions to the parties, not just individual leaders. So it's an entire operation.*

MS: *And this is grassroots politics we are talking about.*

CM: *By the time you get down to Washington you've got Bob Dole flying on a Chiquita Banana airplane to the presidential primaries. Right? By the time it gets up to Washington, it is total corporate domination of the system.*

MS: *And the gravy train rolls on... destination Washington. The capital of capitals, where it finally disgorges its cargo of happy, happy, happy passengers.*

(Music playing while drunk passengers disembark, stumbling and dancing to a Dixieland band)

My observations in the *New York Times* and on "Sixty Minutes" were never intended as criticism of the hard-working municipal officials who participate in the process. One thing I have learned having had the privilege of working in local government is how hard working, honest and dedicated most municipal officials are.

Many local officials called me after the show to say they supported my efforts to reform the system. Tangible reforms resulted from these efforts. Immediately following the broadcast of the "Sixty Minutes" story, the New Jersey League of Municipalities — the association representing local elected officials — implemented measures to ensure that never again would some of the abuses revealed on "Sixty Minutes" occur. A letter from its Executive Director, dated May 13, 1996, said the League is "gratified that [these problems] have been brought to our attention. In fact, the League has clarified its policy on promotional give-aways. Beginning immediately, potential exhibitors are required to certify that they are familiar with the Local Government Ethics Law and the Local Public Contract Law. Further, they must agree to offer no cash (or cash equivalent) prizes."

Although grateful that I helped make the system in New Jersey a bit more open and democratic, I know there is a great deal more work to be done. The junkets I witnessed are amateur events compared to super-charged national political partying and lobbying.

Consider the 1996 Republican National convention in San Diego, California. The city lost the convention in 1972 because of a fund-raising scandal involving ITT corporation. The company had tried to torpedo a pending anti-trust action while tendering a $400,000 contribution to underwrite the Republican convention. Two years later Congress voted to allow taxpayer funding of political conventions. But the fact that taxpayers shelled out $12.4 million to fund the 1996 Republican convention didn't stop big corporate interests from spending millions more on a non-stop party. As the *Wall Street Journal* put it: "ITT's 1972 largess wouldn't even buy 10 seats in the host committee's sky box[in 1996]."

United Airlines, the official carrier of the convention, curried favor by sponsoring parties, booths, hospitality suites, and special events. You name it, corporate lobbyists underwrote it. Conventioneers swooned to oldies singer Frankie Avalon and sampled: golf tournaments, clambakes, fishing trips, museum visits, yacht cruises, and private club parties. How about a fashion show at Saks Fifth Avenue, a private tour of the San Diego Zoo, or a luncheon cruise aboard the yacht Lord Hornblower? In all, corporate interests paid $50 million just for the convention, in addition to record amounts given to federal campaigns.

Many industries additionally hosted private parties for the elected officials who regulate their industries. The Securities industry "honored" the chair of the House Banking Committee with a special party, while Union Pacific Railroad held a special dinner for the House Transportation Committee Chair aboard a refurbished twelve-car luxury business class train circa 1930. (The train was parked near the convention on a special rail spur, built just for the occasion.) General Motors organized a $250,000 lunch for Newt Gingrich.

(The 1996 Democratic convention in Chicago set a

similar tone; United Airlines was also the official carrier and Democratic party planners circulated a list of millions of dollars of "sponsorship opportunities" to big donors, including baseball tickets, theatre tickets, and $150,000 to host a donor dinner party.)

Nothing could match the grand finale of the Republican convention, designed to fete Republican national chairman Haley Barbour. The "Melee for Haley" barbecue relied on the largesse of corporate America to slake the appetites of thousands of rowdy conventioneers. Drinks were on the Big Boys: Seagram Co., Miller Brewing Co., Coca-Cola Co. and Philip Morris Cos. Meanwhile, the National Corn Growers Association delivered 10,000 sumptuous ears and the National Pork Producers Council supplied thirty-seven boxes of ribs so that Republicans could inaugurate the campaign season by chomping on half a ton of free pork. Even the *Wall Street Journal*, hardly a champion of government reform, observed: "The events unfolding here offer tangible evidence of how completely unregulated the campaign-finance system has become. Watergate-era reforms have been rendered all but meaningless by lax enforcement, loose interpretations and recent court decisions that are increasingly hostile to government regulation of politics. The conventions also show how dependent the parties have become on huge corporate donations, even though they were supposed to have been banned from federal campaigns years ago."

Beyond junkets, conventions, lobbying and corporate contributions, the entire scheme of financing politics in America has taken on a surreal, relentless cast. Since the "Sixty Minutes" piece aired, it has become even more evident to the American public that the financing of elections in America undermines our democracy. (The 1998, 1996, and 1994 elections were each the most expensive in history, at the time.) The FBI, the Justice Department and several congressional committees all have open-ended investigations into campaign funding improprieties.

Both major political parties have admitted to taking improper foreign contributions, and returned them. The chairmen of both major political parties have admitted on national television that the campaign financing system in the country is broken, that there are essentially no rules governing the funding of campaigns. (This is not to mention the millions spent by corporations to create phony "grass roots" organizations to press corporate interests.)

This corroborates my personal experience as a practicing politician. Virtually every night in New Jersey there is another fundraiser for another elected official. Politics revolves around these gatherings. I see no barriers to money from corporate coffers and wealthy individuals flowing to politicians.

It is all one relentless national money chase:

- The typical U.S. Senator must count on raising $12,000 a week for re-election. Some Senators need $22,000 per day. Diane Feinstein, whose family has $30 million available to spend on her races, nonetheless spends most of her time raising funds. If Feinstein Inc. were a business, its projected revenues would place it among the top 50 U.S. corporations. "My people want me to be on the phone all the time," she told the *Wall Street Journal.* Most candidates spend upwards of 80 percent of their time raising funds.

- Total population of Little Rock, Arkansas: 158,000; total population of lobbyists in Washington D.C.: 80,000.

- The $500 billion Savings and Loan Bailout, which resulted from banking special interests controlling the political process, could have financed every federal election for well over 500 years.

- Archer Daniels Midland Company and the ethanol industry would not exist without an estimated $6 billion in taxpayer subsidies that former Senator Robert Dole established twenty years ago. ADM became Mr. Dole's most generous political supporter, contributing almost $230,000 to Mr. Dole, who frequently flew on ADM jets.

- In the 1996 Presidential campaign, Dole flew to campaign appearances in planes owned by Lindner family corporate interests; the Lindner family controls the Chiquita banana company. In addition to the airplane, the company gave thousands to then Senator Dole who frequently proposed legislation that would impose harsh trade sanctions on Costa Rica and Ecuador unless they pulled out of a trade deal that diminished Chiquita's banana exports to Europe. No American jobs were involved.

- Currently, roughly 900,000 Americans give $200 or more to campaigns. The needs of .03 percent of the population are put above the other 99.7 percent who don't contribute. Why should the 900,000 Americans that give $200 or more to campaigns have their voices heard over the 269,600,000 citizens who don't contribute? If we are to honor the principle of one person, one vote rather than one dollar, several votes, we must level the playing field.

- There are over $167 billion dollars of corporate welfare subsidies in the federal budget that would not exist except for special interest peddling that the current system of campaign finance allows.

The perpetual national money chase is morally corrosive, undemocratic, distracting and alien to the noblest aspirations of the Founding Fathers. The purpose of government, according to Thomas Jefferson, is "to counteract the power of the moneyed interests." Today, government bows to corporate interests. Polls reveal that people believe that special interests have more say in Washington than ordinary Americans do. Why participate, the people wonder, if the insurance corporations, the tobacco lobby, the savings and loan owners and the industrial polluters run the show?

Citizen involvement in the democratic process is so debilitated that a majority of the population, typically, does not bother to vote. America has the lowest rate of participation of any western industrial democracy.

Individuals aren't the problem. The system is.

Every elected official, every staff member, and every precinct captain is caught in the maw of a perpetual money machine that leaves almost no time for the important business of governing: enacting legislation, planning, thinking and creating. The system forces politicians to become full-time beggars rather than full-time thinkers.

The most humble citizen should have as much influence in running the country as the most well-heeled. In the words of Daniel Webster, as paraphrased by Abraham Lincoln, our government must be "of the people, by the people and for the people."

Many of my friends and colleagues suggested that it would be politically dangerous to speak the truth about the political system in print or on "Sixty Minutes". I understood this. But silence is not acceptable in the face of massive challenges to our democracy. I'd rather lose an election than fail to tell the truth to the people.

All of us have an obligation to embed the concept of justice under the law into our political system. I have had the great fortune to be able to work for many years on campaign finance reform, writing newspaper articles, opinion pieces, law journal articles, and testifying before Congress. I have seen more defeats than victories but the great glory in life is not never falling down, but always getting up once you have fallen. The fight to make our system of government more just and accountable will be won in the long run.

I wrote this book to explain to the people the erosion of our democracy by the current system of campaign financing and favor-mongering. It is not enough to say that the system is morally corrosive and antithetical to our democratic heritage. I want my fellow citizens to understand that this system is costly to them in a tangible sense. There is a hidden legalized graft tax that all of us pay. It is the most expensive tax in America, more costly than anything in society and it affecting the way each one of us lives every day. It drains our pocketbooks, damages our natural environment, and changes the character of our neighborhoods and communities. In New Jersey it is the Garden State Shakedown.

My twenty years of experience in politics tells me that virtually every important issue — the environment, taxes, over-development, guns, crime, privacy etc. — comes down to a question of corporate interest money. Suburban residents feel enormous frustration with sprawl, runaway development, and traffic congestion but they don't associate these problems with the control the real estate and development lobbies have in Trenton and in Washington. They should, because these private actors have much more power over how New Jersey communities are shaped than the communities themselves.

In New Jersey, there is massive frustration that automobile insurance rates are the highest in the country. Multiple explanations are advanced, but the debate rarely centers on the fact that insurance companies collaborate on prices and have unusual say in the political process. States that are not as tightly in the grip of the insurance lobby have achieved substantial savings and reform.

Similarly, many Garden State residents decry the fact that the state has more toxic waste sites than any state in the nation and that 85 percent of New Jersey's waterways are neither swimmable nor fishable; rarely, however, does the political debate center around the enormous power of the polluter lobby in Trenton and Washington.

New Jersey taxes are so high, not just because of inefficiency or runaway government spending, but because of the Garden State Graft Tax. Consider, for example, the expensive and costly incinerators that dot New Jersey's landscape. Municipalities are paying twice the market rate to dispose of garbage because incinerator companies and investment bankers pressured the political system to build these behemoths. In the mid-1990's a handful of Wall Street investment banks donated more than $288,000 to both political parties in New Jersey. These same firms received over $56 million in fees for underwriting billions in state bonds that were floated to back the incinerators. None of these fees was awarded on a competitive basis. Now taxpayers are bailing out these failed projects, in effect paying to poison themselves. No democratic decision making process would ever have arrived at this outcome, but when the corporate interests are in charge, the citizens pay. Taxes are high because contributors to the political system expect goodies in return.

Citizens and communities ultimately pay in more than lucre for political graft. The values of the society and the next generation are shaped by a rigged system. Because of the tight control of corporate interests, political discourse itself is highly restricted. In political campaigns there is rarely any mention of corporate crime, even though the FBI estimates that burglary and robbery combined cost the United States approximately $4 billion a year while white collar fraud costs $200 billion a year. There is rarely any mention of corporate welfare which takes up $167 billion of the federal budget each year, even as individual welfare is central to most campaigns.

This books explains how the Garden State Shakedown works and what we can do about it. Other states have enacted sweeping campaign finance reform measures and dramatically improved their democratic systems. So can New Jersey. Throughout American history episodes of fundamental reform have followed periods of dark corruption; at times New Jersey led the way in this rebirth. The state can be a leader again, and it must be.

CHAPTER TWO

TROUBLE IN THE HEARTLAND

"All the politics that are in me, I learned in New Jersey."
— Woodrow Wilson

While life is good for the corporate lobbyists riding the "Gravy Train", life is not always so easy for residents of the Garden State.

I will never forget campaigning one hot summer night in May 1996 in a suburb near New Brunswick. A women answered the door in a modest brick ranch house. She was middle-aged, with gray hair and deep lines in her face; she was dignified but appeared shaken. At first she seemed reluctant to talk, but gradually she revealed that her primary concern is the environment of New Jersey. Her son, diagnosed with leukemia, had passed away a year earlier. What bothered her, she related to me as she began to cry softly, is that six other children in her immediate neighborhood had also contracted leukemia and she was sure it was linked to the hazardous waste superfund site located only a few hundred yards from her house. She had repeatedly told authorities of the smell coming from the site but years had passed with no clean-up.

Her story, and many others I have heard, speak to deep concerns about the quality of life in New Jersey. Many Garden State residents say: we must have a strange view of prosperity if the air we breathe and the water we drink are endangered, if we must sit in traffic all day, if utility and other rates rise faster than the rate of inflation, and if education costs and property taxes spiral out of control.

In recent years, political pundits have been mystified as to why the electorate in New Jersey has been so focused on auto insurance premiums. Apart from the importance of the automobile to life in New Jersey, the issue is symbolic of deeper concerns that residents have about life in the Garden State. To say that New Jersey residents pay the highest auto insurance and property taxes in the country is only to scratch the surface of the Suburban Squeeze that many New Jerseyans find themselves in. Despite certain positive economic indicators, a declining quality of life in this state has produced unusual dissatisfaction.

There are severe problems with New Jersey's environment. New Jersey has over 8,000 hazardous waste sites, more than any state in the nation. One hundred percent of Garden State waterways are classified as "threatened" by the state Department of Environmental Protection and New Jersey's air pollution levels are the nation's second worst. These environmental factors may well be responsible for marked increases in childhood cancer and childhood asthma. New Jersey has the second highest incidence of breast cancer in the nation, and scientists are increasingly looking at environmental factors.

New Jersey has the second-worst air quality in the nation after the Los Angeles metropolitan area. Air pollution prematurely claims the lives of 1,500 New Jersey citizens every year. "Air pollution is causing an epidemic of disease in New Jersey," says Dr. Irwin Berlin, the director of Pulmonary Medicine at St. Elizabeth hospital. On one out of every three days in summer, smog reaches unhealthy levels and emergency room admissions for asthma jump by 26 percent statewide. More than asthma patients suffer. Roughly 900,000 Garden State residents suffer from respiratory diseases, such as emphysema, bronchitis and pneumonia, all of which are aggravated by air pollutants. Despite this, a loophole in the state law allows two of the most powerful companies in the state, PSE&G and Atlantic Electric to operate power plants that don't meet modern Clean Air Act standards. As a consequence, four power plants operated by these companies emit over 90 percent of the worst air pollutants in the state including mercury, nitrogen oxide, and sulfur dioxide. Having spent $1.4 million on lobbyists and campaign contributions from 1994 to 1997, these companies continue to fight to keep their antiquated, polluting plants open.

Environmental problems in the vastly underprivileged urban areas of New Jersey are many times more severe. According to the EPA, one in six children have unacceptable levels of lead in their blood. Half of all inner-city children in New Jersey may be lead poisoned. (High levels of lead can lead to seizures, comas, damage to the nervous and kidney systems, and even death.) Often, incinerator companies choose to site environmentally dangerous incinerators near urban centers.

New Jerseyans can't escape the Suburban Squeeze in their own homes. While paying the highest property tax rates in the nation, New Jerseyans have seen the values of their homes decline to the point where New Jersey has the third highest percentage in the nation of household mortgages in foreclosure. Many New Jersey households have difficulty educating their children; indeed, the cost of tuition at state colleges in New Jersey is the highest in the nation.

It also costs more to run homes in New Jersey. New Jersey has the fourth highest utility rates in the country, with an average cost of 9 cents per kilowatt hour, much higher than the national average of 5 cents per kilowatt hour. In some New Jersey communities senior citizens pay one quarter to one third of their annual social security checks just to cover the cost of utilities. Seniors are struggling to pay their $400 to $500 per month bill because the current Administration allows utilities to pass along the costs of nuclear power plants that are shut for safety violations.

Increases in water utility rates have risen much faster than the rate of inflation in the last five years and a recent study by the New Jersey Public Interest Research Group found — you guessed it — that New Jerseyans pay the highest bank fees of any state in the nation for the privilege of using our own money. (In the mid-1990's, bankruptcies in New Jersey hit an all-time high, almost 28,000, and New Jersey had the distinction of becoming the state with the highest median amount for people filing bankruptcy, nearly $66,000 in 1995. Apart from the influence of Atlantic City, many New Jersey credit analysts blame the increase in extensive credit. A credit counselor in New Jersey was called by a women in distress because her 12 year old daughter had just received a credit card from a major retail clothing chain that targets youthful clientele.)

The car offers no refuge from the spiraling costs of home ownership and environmental degradation.

Suburban sprawl and endless traffic have only gotten worse. New Jersey is the most densely populated state in the country. This isn't an accident; the secret about the state's master plan for growth has been out for a long time: there is no plan. I know from my work as a town councilman that developers simply do not pay their fair share of road repairs or education costs or new sewage costs. The result is that towns relentlessly encourage new development which in fact causes taxes to rise, not fall, because the costs of new sewers, roads and schools are so great.

If New Jerseyans feel a Suburban Squeeze, the situation in urban New Jersey is even more alarming. Camden, for example, is the poorest city for its size in the nation — more destitute than cities in Mississippi and Alabama. The infant mortality rate in Camden is higher than in some Third World countries and the school dropout rate is 70 percent. There is considerable urban poverty in New Jersey; one out of ten citizens lives below the poverty line and each night almost 300,000 New Jersey children go to bed hungry. New Jersey also receives less per dollar sent to Washington than any other state in the nation, so there is not much federal help for the urban poor.

If an insurance company wants a rate increase or a casino mogul wants a tunnel built, the government is only too willing to oblige. But when it comes to improving New Jersey's quality of life, there is precious little relief for middle class and poor citizens of New Jersey. Although New Jersey residents may feel these problems more acutely than residents of other states, the quality of life problems in New Jersey are spreading to many communities around the nation.

Conventional wisdom is that suburbs face a different set of problems than America's cities. The reality is that suburbs are consumed with many of the same problems. Although the suburbs appear more stable than urban areas, the nomadic uncertainty of contemporary corporate life brings many of the same uncertainties to the suburbs as to the city. Historian Frederick Jackson Turner wrote about the closing of the American frontier at the end of the Nineteenth Century and how that profoundly changed American politics. At the end of the Twentieth Century, the suburban frontier is also beginning to close as cities, suburbs and ex-urban areas blur together. The country is beginning to face one uniform set of problems, often having to do with quality of life.

The closing of the suburban frontier at the end of the twentieth century is as profound a shift in American politics as the closing of the frontier at the end of the nineteenth. New Jersey is the most suburban state in the nation — 84 percent of the population lives in the suburbs — and political problems here portend much about the future of the nation.

As suggested in the previous chapter, many quality of life problems in New Jersey stem from the overwhelming power of corporate special interests. The real estate, chemical, utility, insurance, and banking industries have a much greater say in the direction of suburban life than the citizens. The following chapters explain how this power affects the daily lives of Garden State citizens.

CHAPTER THREE

PRUDENTIAL'S TENTACLES AROUND YOUR WALLET.

"The Prudential wove a network of money tentacles that stretched from end to end of the state of New Jersey and made its officers the most powerful men in the community, able to dictate to the executives at Trenton, and to make and unmake governors."

— Prudential Insurance Corporation Official History (1975) quoting an unidentified newspaper regarding Prudential's influence subsequent to its founding in 1875.

It's more expensive to insure an automobile in New Jersey than in any other state in the Union, with rates averaging $1,000 per motorist. The issue is so rancorous that it has dominated the Governor's race for the last decade and has led to rallies, protests and thousands of people driving without insurance. The industry offers a battery of reasons that explain the high auto insurance premiums in New Jersey: too many lawyers, too crowded a state, too much fraud, etc. None of these theories explains the problem.

The real reason that rates are so high is that New Jersey doesn't have enough democracy and the insurance companies have too much power. One company in particular, Prudential, wields enormous power over state government, and New Jersey consumers are paying for this special access and influence.

Compared to other states, New Jersey positively coddles the insurance industry. Other states have received significant rate relief because the citizens have voted in referenda to lower rates and to prevent insurance companies from passing along bloated costs to consumers. (In New Jersey, the political parties and their corporate sponsors have steadfastly refused to grant the citizenry this fundamental democratic tool.)

In California, for example, voters in a referendum passed an auto insurance reduction plan that has saved California motorists approximately $15 billion since

1988. The rollbacks and reforms approved by California voters ten years ago have been upheld as constitutional by the state's Supreme Court and the U.S. Supreme Court and have had a dramatic impact upon California's auto insurance system, once the second most costly in the nation. The insurance industry doesn't want New Jersey consumers to know that premium rollbacks and other reforms are constitutional and have produced huge savings on the other side of the country.

But it does work. Proposition 103 — the ballot measure approved by California voters despite an expenditure of $80 million against it by the insurance industry — mandated a 20 percent rollback in auto, homeowner, and business premiums. The measure also instituted stringent controls on insurance company profiteering, waste and inefficiency, required insurers to base auto insurance premiums on driving safety record rather than zip code, and mandated a 20 percent good driver discount. Here are the results (data are from annual published reports of the National Association of Insurance Commissioners).

- Over $1.18 billion in refunds, averaging $200 per motorist, have been paid to California motorists under the 103 rollback requirement.

- Because of a freeze on rates imposed pursuant to 103's authority during the legal challenges to the measure, California motorists have saved an additional $14.7 billion on private passenger automobile insurance since 1990.

- The average auto liability insurance premium

decreased by 4.5 percent in California between 1989 and 1994; the average premium throughout the rest of the nation increased 29.6 percent in the same period.

- The average auto liability insurance premium decreased by 0.1 percent in California between 1989 and 1995, while the average premium throughout the rest of the nation increased 32.2 percent.

- In 1988, California had the seventh fastest rate of annual growth in auto insurance liability premiums in the nation. By 1994, California was 47th. Between 1988 and 1994, California experienced the slowest rate of auto premium growth of any state.

- In 1989, California had the second highest average liability premium in the nation. In 1994, it ranked 12th. In 1995, 11th.

Proposition 103 forced insurance companies to tighten their belts: cut commissions, reduce expenses, fight fraud, and improve loss prevention. As a result, the number of auto accident lawsuits filed in California Superior Courts dropped 45 percent since 1988. And auto insurance continues to be highly profitable in the state, notwithstanding the requirements of Proposition 103.

A core reason that there has not been fundamental reform of the auto insurance laws in New Jersey, despite the issue's importance in every gubernatorial contest in the last ten years, is that there is no arms-length relationship between the government and the insurance industry in New Jersey. In a unique arrangement, six of the 23 members of Prudential's board of directors are appointed by the state's chief justice. These appointees have included several of New Jersey's former governors, including one who spent 11 years on Prudential's board after leaving office. It was little surprise, then, when in 1994 state regulators let the company investigate itself when motorists and insurance agents complained that Prudential and two other insurance companies were telling some customers that their auto insurance policies would be canceled unless they bought other lines of insurance. State regulators investigated the allegations against the two small out-of-state companies but allowed Prudential to conduct its own investigation. The regulators exonerated Prudential after it hired a subcontractor to perform a customer survey, which found only several isolated incidents of forced sales.

Although Prudential might get a little extra-special help in New Jersey, the state has been generous to the entire industry. The State's Insurance Department has seen fit to grant eight separate rate increases since 1994 to various auto insurers, not including the annual cost-of-living increases that all insurers impose on drivers. Indeed, a State Department of Insurance survey shows that many North Jersey residents saw double digit annual increases in their premiums during the 1990's.

Soft treatment of insurance companies extends to many different types of insurance, not just auto. For example, in 1995 when New Jersey insurance regulators announced the fruits of a multi-state investigation of Prudential Insurance Co., they presented it as a consumer victory. Prudential would pay a record $ 35-million fine, they said, as well as restitution of up to one billion dollars to thousands of customers who might have been cheated by rogue sales agents. The complaints, which have also been leveled against other major insurance companies, involve a practice known as "churning," in which agents visit longtime, often elderly, customers, and persuade them to turn in or borrow from their existing policies. The money from the old policy is then used to buy a policy with a higher cash value. In their lawsuits, the customers say the agents told them that they would not have to pay higher premiums. But after a few years, the customers faced unexpected bills or found that their policies had lapsed.

In recent years, Prudential Insurance has been rocked by several scandals. The lawsuits by life insurance policyholders came soon after Prudential's securities-brokerage division paid $1.5 billion to settle cases with customers who had invested in risky limited partnerships that later collapsed. Company brokers had misleadingly sold the partnerships as safe investments. A federal judge overseeing the life insurance case fined Prudential $1 million after the company admitted destroying documents and evidence.

Critics contend, however, that the deal struck with Prudential (largely at the request of the state of New Jersey) was a turkey. Florida's Insurance Commissioner was blunt: he called the settlement a "bad deal" that "does not begin to compensate Florida's consumers, whose pockets were picked." In addition, most customers who lost money may never get it back because the settlement, largely based on proposals by Prudential, puts a heavy burden of proof on the customers. It was "a white-wash," said J. Bruce Miller, a Kentucky lawyer who represents Prudential customers and former agents suing the company. The highly-touted settlement makes it difficult or impossible for many aggrieved customers to get their money back. The deal's terms, said the Massachusetts attorney general's office, are even less generous than what Prudential had already offered individual customers on its own.

Many claim that the multistate probe of Prudential led by New Jersey was instigated at Prudential's request and designed to reach a weak settlement that would benefit the company. Indeed, New Jersey held off probing Prudential for many years after complaints about churning started turning up in the mid-1980's. The probe ignored major areas of alleged wrongdoing by Prudential and, for example, ignored an internal company memo admitting that the company engaged in massive churning nationwide and that senior management knew about it. The probe also failed to investigate a statement from an agent that the company had back-dated documents. "What they did was not an investigation," said Florida's Insurance Commissioner.

Ultimately, the only solution to rising auto and other insurance rates will be to subject the insurance industry to the same type of regulation that other financial firms like banks and securities houses face — federal regulation. Right now the insurance industry is a monstrous $750 billion industry that, unlike banking and securities, has managed to remain free of federal regulation, an exemption written into federal law in 1945.

Meanwhile, at the state level, insurers — as big employers and generous campaign contributors — always receive soft treatment. The only organization with a pretense to co-ordinating national regulation of insurance companies is the National Association of Insurance Commissioners. Founded in 1871 to help regulators from different states devise common approaches, the organization relies for funding almost exclusively on the industry. The organization almost began to scrutinize the industry in the mid-1980's when a number of insurance firms failed. But when the industry threatened to boycott the organization, it dropped plans to require car and homeowners insurers to report claims data by zip code, which would have enabled closer review of rates and sales practices. The organization also abandoned an effort to establish a computer system that would require insurers to file new policies and rates electronically.

Despite the fact that insurance companies operate in all fifty states and around the globe, and that mergers are creating multibillion dollars behemoths, the insurance industry remains regulated only by the states. Estimates are that the 50 states combined spend on insurance regulation less than one-third of what the federal government spends to regulate the banking industry. Missouri Insurance Commissioner Jay Angoff says state regulation has survived because the insurance companies want it. As he told the *Wall Street Journal*: "They'd rather be regulated by 50 monkeys than one big gorilla."

The way to reduce auto and other rates for New Jersey consumers is to repeal the 1945 federal loophole that allows insurance companies to escape federal regulation, including anti-trust laws. As long as these companies can collude on prices, our rates will continue to rise. New Jerseyans also need initiative and referendum so they can rollback rates the way California citizens did.

Until these fundamental reforms occur, New Jersey residents will continue to pay the New Jersey Graft Tax and consumers will be victims of the Garden State Shakedown.

CHAPTER FOUR

TOXIC WASTE AND NEW JERSEY:
PERFECT TOGETHER?

"Nature can do more than physicians."
— Oliver Cromwell

What a great idea! Let's build an enormous garbage-burning incinerator and charge taxpayers twice the market rate for disposing of trash. Let's put this project next to the poorest neighborhood in the most populated city in the county. And if it doesn't work, let's have the taxpayers bail out the project.

This was the "logic" behind building incinerators throughout New Jersey. The result everywhere is the same: the projects are unmitigated disasters that either are never built or, once built, charge twice the market rate and can't find customers. The state is now asking every taxpayer in the state to bail out these White Elephants. Logic did not create these projects. Raw political power did. The incinerator companies and the investment banks that drove these projects benefitted enormously; the public is still paying the tab. The battle over incinerators is a textbook example of how New Jerseyans repeatedly pay a Garden State Shakedown Tax to subsidize the destruction of their own environment.

In the mid 1980's, incinerator companies and Wall Street bankers conceived of a plan to build a trash incinerator in my home county of Mercer. The politicians and the political parties benefitted handsomely from payments made by these companies. Although there are very rural areas in Mercer County, the plan called for building the project near the City of Trenton, the county's most populous and impecunious neighborhood.

Ogden-Martin corporation, the same company that was involved in the Mercer County incinerator, built an incinerator in Lake County, Florida, over the objections of local residents. Consider a typical letter printed in the local paper after the incinerator came on-line: "I'm extremely concerned about what they are burning in the plant. We live about one mile away and both my daughter and I have chronic sinus and respiratory problems ... We never had any such problems in the past... Whatever is being burned in the plant is not safe, is polluting the air and water, and is slowly killing my family and others over a period of years."

Consider another letter from a resident living near Ogden-Martin's Florida incinerator: "I'm 18 miles away and when the wind blows this way, it makes me ill. That plant should be closed." I even had a County supervisor from Florida place an unsolicited call to warn me, as an elected official, that the worst decision he had made in public life was to vote for an incinerator; he urged me to reject it in New Jersey.

The plan was to use the incinerator of Mercer County as a kind of garbage Mecca for the rest of New Jersey; it would accept trash from many different counties. Ogden-Martin didn't deny that toxic substances are burned in incinerators. The company argued that the amounts burned are safe. Many scientists and doctors disagree. (An Ogden-Martin project in Canada was canceled recently when a group of local doctors signed a letter detailing the health hazards of incineration. In general, Ogden-Martin is no paragon of environmental responsibility. In one year, the company was cited for 7,000 violations of federal environmental laws by the EPA in addition to state violations.)

Incinerators emit an array of toxic and carcinogenic chemicals including toxic heavy metals (such as lead, cadmium, mercury and arsenic), and dangerous organic compounds such as dioxin and PCBs. The incinerator ash frequently contains four times as much mercury and three times as much lead as permissible under federal drinking water standards. The residue from incineration is highly toxic; there is no way to dispose of it safely, and the net effect of incineration is simply to create another hazardous waste site.

Apart from the daily environmental problems associated with incinerators, proponents of the incinerator never addressed the problem of what happens when an incineration plant malfunctions. Apparently this occurs from time to time, as an *Associated Press* article of February 8, 1994 suggests. The story reported that an incinerator in Albany, New York malfunctioned and "caused a shower of unburned oil particles to darken the snow-covered ground in downtown Albany..."

Quite apart from the health arguments, incinerators are White Elephants that represent the most expensive method of disposing of garbage known to humankind.

As the *Wall Street Journal* reports communities around the country regret having built garbage facilities: "Officials paid little mind to the economics of burning trash. Very simply, the current economics are terrible, requiring residential and commercial customers — as well as taxpayers — to pay hundreds of millions of dollars a year over and above the going market rate for trash disposal. The average incinerator's disposal fee is $56 a ton, twice the $28 average at dumps." The *Journal* concludes that: "The garbage crisis, though it appealed perfectly to the nation's collective guilt over throwing away so much stuff, was more fiction than fact."

Cities and counties across the United States are abandoning incineration projects because the economics of the industry has changed so drastically that incineration is no longer the most cost-effective method of trash disposal. According to the *Engineering News-Record*, "less waste generation and more public opposition have combined to constrict the market for future solid-waste-to-energy plants, according to a new industry survey. The number of planned incinerators has dropped by more than 50 percent since 1991." In a comprehensive survey, released by an industry publication, an industry analyst observed: "The so-called waste disposal crises in the Northeast did not materialize and many area landfills continue to operate charging relatively low tipping fees..." Why would elected representatives ever commit us to build a massive, expensive and dangerous incinerator adjacent to a populated neighborhood? There is no logical, rational or public interest explanation. But Ogden-Martin spent thousands hiring lobbyists to convince elected officials to commit our tax dollars to build incinerators. And the other groups profiting from the planned Mercer incinerator — investment bankers and lawyers — also contributed heavily. Certainly, these groups have greater access to power and more influence than the ordinary American affected by such projects.

Here's how the deal works. After urging from the incineration companies and bankers, our elected officials decide that we need an incinerator. (Even though studies show that recycling can handle the problem). The officials then agree to raise millions of dollars by issuing debt in the name of taxpayers: $200 million in the case of the proposed Mercer County incinerator. From this taxpayer money Ogden-Martin, the bankers, and the lawyers are paid up front. The taxpayer bears the risk. These private parties get the benefit. Even though currently legal, the deal presents severe conflicts of interest because the lawyers and bankers do not bid competitively to represent us taxpayers. Instead, it appears as if they are chosen because they make political contributions.

Bankers, lawyers and other experts raked in almost $12 million of our tax dollars on the Mercer County incinerator before even one brick had been laid. A New York investment bank on the project was one of the top ten contributors to candidates and parties in New Jersey; all of the Wall Street banks involved in the proposed incinerator were also big political contributors. (The fee arrangement with Wall Street banks amounted to an extraordinary 2.5 percent of the proposed $250 million cost of the project; another $7,327,138 million of taxpayer money was spent on various law firms, realtors and other consultants before anything was built.)

It is a complete waste of taxpayer dollars to award contracts to Wall Street investment banks without requiring bids. Any homeowner in the country would take bids from various banks if they wanted to borrow money to buy a house. The least government can do is follow this elementary principle of finance when borrowing money in the taxpayers name to finance an incinerator.

For the companies, however, this is an unbeatable investment: bankers give tens of thousands of dollars to the political process; in turn, they receive multi-million dollar projects and fees.

Despite all the environmental, financial, and conflict of interest problems with building an incinerator in Mercer country, the proponents of the plan soldiered on for over ten years to get the project built. At times the battle was comical: the county agency responsible for building the incinerator at one point hired a public relations firm — with taxpayer money — to convince taxpayers that they really wanted an enormously expensive and environmentally dangerous project in their backyard. The credibility of the county agency fighting for the incinerator was diminished considerably when the agency head admitted in writing that an employee had used an agency car, paid for by the taxpayer, to frequent a Pennsylvania Go-Go bar.

The Mercer County incinerator was presented to the citizenry as a *fait accompli*. Every newspaper editorial board favored it, every major business group lined up behind it, and no politician dared oppose it. The only people fighting the project were a handful of environmental groups and committed citizens. We labored on for a ten year period, attending public political meetings, lengthy hearings, agency proceedings, caucuses, strategy sessions and meetings with leaders and scientists. Gradually, it became clear that the project was a boondoggle. Incinerators that had already been built around the state lost more and more money as it became clear that every other option for trash disposal is less expensive than incineration. The economics of these projects became so bad that the state was asked to intercede to bail-out the counties. Nobody could account for the enormous expenditure of taxpayer money before even a brick was laid.

Finally, in 1996, the Mercer County incineration project was canceled. Since that time, more incinerators around the state have failed or needed state bailouts. (The State Legislature has been busily crafting a plan to have the taxpayer bail out all incinerator projects throughout the state.)

Wherever these incinerators are put to a vote, they fail. The truth is that operating incinerators have caused both economic and environmental problems in communities around the country. Their record is so bad that incinerators have been canceled across America.

Show me a subsidy, and I will show you pollution. The entire technology of incineration would not exist without massive government subsidies. Unfortunately, under our system of special interest dominance, this is all too common. This is particularly unfortunate when cancer rates among children rise, and experts believe that a growing exposure to new chemicals in the environment is the culprit. A child in the United States faces a one in 600 risk of contracting cancer by age 10; each year 8,000 children below the age of 15 contact cancer. Cancer is the most common form of fatal childhood disease, accounting for about 10 percent of all deaths. The rate of increase of children's cancer has been roughly one percent a year according to the National Cancer Institute, meaning that over a few decades there has been a startling double-digit increase.

In place of incineration, we need increased recycling and other measures that would reduce waste at the source. Studies conducted by the Congressional Office of Technology Assessment and the Environmental Protection Agency show that America produces, per capita, twice as much waste as any other country on Earth, and we recycle at half the rate that European nations do.

Some communities in America have taken aggressive action to improve recycling efforts and some communities, like Seattle, Washington, recycle up to 80 percent of their waste. (The figure is 90 percent in Germany and Japan.) Surely we can do a better job of reducing waste at the source and recycling.

The challenge is to enact federal laws — like a ban on incinerators — that serve the taxpayer and the environment. Other countries, like Australia, have enacted national bans on incinerators for both environmental and economic reasons. My experience with the proposed Mercer county incinerator convinces me that we need a similar ban here at the federal level. By reforming the system of campaign financing and lobbying, we can forestall expensive and wasteful projects like incinerators.

CHAPTER FIVE

THE GARDEN STATE BECOMES THE CEMENT STATE

*"If the real estate gang could,
they would raise the rents in the graveyard."*
— Frank Dane

New Jersey has a bizarre infrastructure topography that is a monument to the automobile and to unplanned development. If you want to turn left, you turn right (on something called a "jughandle"). If you want to drive North, you take I-295 South; if you want to drive South, you take I-95 North. If you live in South Brunswick, you get your mail in Neshanic Station. If you live in South Brunswick, you get your mail addressed to Monmouth Junction. If you live in Lawrenceville or West Windsor, your mail comes addressed to Princeton. In fact, if you live anywhere in Central New Jersey, you might have a Princeton address. Even the federal post office can't keep up with helter-skelter development in New Jersey. Most developments have names like Whispering Woods or Gentle Pines or Babbling Brook and undoubtedly they once were.

The suburban quality of life is under siege. Suburban residents daily confront massive sprawl, interminable traffic, diminishing Open Space, and the highest property taxes in the country. All of these problems result from helter-skelter development, poor planning, and the power of the real estate, transportation and trucking lobbies.

Consider one quality of life threat with deadly implications: eighteen-wheel, forty-ton trucks that daily rattle down the residential, local roads of Central New Jersey. The trucks are here because this is the only region on the East Coast where I-95 is not continuous;

rather than pay the tolls on the New Jersey Turnpike, these behemoths roll down the local roads of Central New Jersey — through residential neighborhoods — with impunity.

Eighteen-wheel trucks depart from major inter-state roadways like I-95, I-287, and the New Jersey Turnpike to continue their long-distance runs on the following state roads: route 31 or route 29 which travel through Hunterdon and Mercer counties; route 206 which travels through Somerset and Mercer counties; route 1 which travels through Mercer and Middlesex Counties; route 130 which travels through Middlesex; and route 9 which travels through Monmouth counties.

This problem has been festering for too long. As long ago as October 1992, twenty-six year old Wendy McMichael died when her car was hit by a 30-ton tractor trailer near Cranbury on Route 130. There have been other fatal and near fatal mishaps involving trucks in Central New Jersey. (Nor is this problem limited to Central New Jersey; all across the nation massive trucks rattle down residential roads to save highway tolls. The danger and cost are significant and the problem will only get worse as the new economy demands more and more deliveries.)

Massive long-haul rigs have no place on the local, residential roads of New Jersey. They create noise problems, traffic problems, and safety problems. It is time to restore peace and quiet to our neighborhoods by having the federal government ban these trucks from the local roads of Central New Jersey. We need a new, federal solution to restore the tranquility of our neighborhoods.

We need a law forbidding any long-haul truck from leaving the New Jersey Turnpike, I-95 or I-287 or I-78 or any other interstate highway unless the trucker can show a manifest indicating a local delivery in New Jersey. The federal government has an interest in promoting the integrity of the interstate highway system, in promoting the tranquility and quietude of the neighborhoods adjacent to federal highways, and, most importantly, in promoting the health and safety of local neighborhoods and of drivers on local roads who too frequently are involved in accidents, many fatal, with 30-ton trucks. This law would subject the offending trucking corporation to a fine double that now imposed for speeding or safety violations on state roads in New Jersey. At the same time, tolls should be lowered on the Turnpike so that hard-working truckers and small businesses do not suffer.

Such a ban would be constitutional because Congress has the authority under the Commerce Clause to regulate the flow of interstate traffic. The federal government could enforce such restrictions on truck traffic by requiring the state of New Jersey to monitor the manifests. If the state of New Jersey failed to monitor truck manifests, the state would no longer be eligible for federal highway money.

Several communities, including Princeton, have made efforts to solve the problem by asking the State to lower speed limits on these roads or by beefing up local enforcement. This has some positive effect, but only a comprehensive federal solution can significantly alleviate the traffic and other problems that this truck traffic generates in New Jersey.

In Princeton, for example, the Princeton Township Committee passed a resolution demanding that the speed limit along route 206 — which travels through Princeton — be reduced. Eventually we were able to lower the speed limit from 45 to 35 miles per hour, which has deterred trucks from coming into town. Princeton Township police have also beefed up enforcement of speed limits and safety violations along 206.

The Committee voted unanimously to authorize and direct the Township Police to increase the patrol and inspection of all vehicles, including trucks, along Route 206. Only the state police have authority to conduct random truck inspections. But, at my urging, the Committee received a legal opinion from Princeton's attorney that indicates that local Township police can stop vehicles for "probable cause." This means trucks can be stopped for brake lights or windshields that do not work, expired inspection stickers, or mufflers that are too loud.

Astoundingly, when the State Police came to Princeton, at our urging, to randomly stop and inspect trucks, they found that 75 percent of the trucks had safety problems like malfunctioning lights or brakes or windshield wipers. Although we have temporarily alleviated the problem in Princeton, it will not be solved without federal action. Other communities around the country and the state will have to cope with similar problems.

When I proposed a federal solution to the trucking problem, the response of the trucking lobby in New Jersey was swift and unequivocal. The chief lobbyist for the trucking industry said it was "un-American and unconstitutional" and suggested that any elected official proposing such a solution should "undergo an IQ test." Of the residents who live adjacent to local roads frequented by trucks, the lobbyist said: "If they don't like it, they can leave."

Until the politicians stand up to the truck lobby, this dangerous problem will continue. In the long run, the only way to alleviate the problem of traffic in suburban New Jersey is to control development. Already, New Jersey is the most densely populated state in the country and although the state professes to have a plan, very little proposed development is ever denied. And developers never pay their fair share of road repairs or education costs or new sewage costs.

The result is a vicious cycle in which towns chase new development because they believe that will add money to the tax rolls; in fact the costs of development substantially outweigh the benefits. The resulting explosion of growth and soaring property taxes diminishes the suburban quality of life and aggravates the traffic problem. It is also an important reason that New Jersey has the highest property taxes in the nation.

One vignette illustrates the power of the real estate lobby in New Jersey. The state is famous for its legion of malls. Many years ago, the owners of these developments decided to prevent citizens from distributing literature or speaking to customers in the malls. (Many private communities in New Jersey have such prohibitions, and it is very hard to find any public space to discuss public issues.) Some New Jersey citizens sued, and the New Jersey Supreme Court ruled that speaking publicly in the malls is protected by the First Amendment. The response of the real estate lobby? The mall owners instituted a requirement that anyone seeking to distribute literature in malls had to take out a one million dollar insurance policy. This was clearly a measure designed to chill free speech. This case also went up to the Supreme Court where the mall owners again lost. It is only a matter of time before the real estate lobby comes up with another gimmick to chill public speech.

Many other suburban states have attacked the problem of sprawl and over-development head on, but not New Jersey where the real estate lobby is perhaps the most powerful in the state. The future configuration of the state is not determined by citizens, but by companies like Hovnanian and Toll Brothers that build massive developments. These developers have tied the hands of many municipalities. Under current law, municipalities are prevented from charging developers for the increases in public works (schools, sewers, roads, etc.) that are needed each time a development arises. As a result, property taxes are continually raised. The situation has become intolerable. Growth can be positive, but it should not come at the expense of those already living in the community.

Communities in New Jersey need the ability to charge "impact fees" so that developers pay the full cost of development, and they need "timed growth ordinances" that allow the community to plan intelligently. Many other states and communities have successfully implemented these programs to stop sprawl. One of the key initiatives involves reversing the process whereby cities and older suburbs in effect subsidize development by subsidizing sewers and other infrastructure for the newer suburbs. States like Maryland have taken the lead and enacted "smart growth" programs that encourage development only in already developed areas.

Many other strategies like downtown revitalization and historic preservation or reclaiming urban brownfield lands also help stem sprawl. In Congress, a Smart Growth Task Force, organized by Oregon Representative Earl Blumenauer, promotes smart growth strategies in an array of federal programs. Federal and state government can also do more to protect and preserve Open Space. One of the most satisfying measures we were able to pass on Princeton Township Committee was a law to preserve a 570 acre tract of land that sits adjacent to Princeton's Revolutionary War Battlefield. The Battle fought there on January 1, 1777 was one of the turning points of the Revolution. Few Revolutionary War battlefields remain in the country, and it was an honor to help protect and preserve one of them. The federal government can do more to protect our heritage and our history and plan our communities by offering incentives to preserve Open Space.

Right now, the opposite is happening in Washington. Developers are pushing bills that would make it easier for companies to challenge local planning and zoning procedures in federal court. These measures are a direct challenge to New Jersey's tradition of home rule and threaten to further undermine the limited planning tools available to New Jersey localities.

CHAPTER SIX

THE GUN LOBBY WANTS MORE GUNS FOR SUBURBAN TEENS

"It is not the violence of the few that concerns me; it is the silence of the many."
— Martin Luther King

On Thursday, November 6, 1997 at 6:23 p.m. an ATM repairman in Princeton calls 911 because, during the course of a routine machine servicing, he sees a female teller with her hands bound in a Summit bank on Nassau Street, the main street in town. The police arrive to find a gunman wearing a ski mask and latex gloves, with his forearm around a woman hostage's neck and a .44-caliber revolver pointed at her head. The gun is loaded with deadly hollow-point bullets. The masked man says his life is over, and starts to count. A police sharpshooter fires, killing the robber, as the horrified woman runs away. A second man in a ski mask and dark clothing escapes, dragging another female hostage. Carrying a semi-automatic weapon known as a Repeater he hijacks a car from a 91-year-old man. The suspect pistol whips the elderly man and throws him from the car. After driving out of the state, he is apprehended days later.

The news accounts of the fatal shooting, typically, reported in elaborate detail the history of the suspects and their possible motivation. But there was hardly any reporting about how two individuals with criminal records obtained an illegal semi-automatic weapon and a .44 caliber revolver. According to the Federal Alcohol, Tobacco and Firearms Bureau, the serial number of the guns had been rubbed off, suggesting the weapons were imported illegally from out of state.

If a quiet, academic community like Princeton can

fall victim to this mayhem, no community in the United States is safe from gun violence. There is no more important issue than reducing the level of violence in society. It is unacceptable anywhere in the country, and increasingly the violence is moving to the suburbs and involves children. Every two hours in this country a child is killed with a loaded gun. There are measures we could enact now to end this scourge.

While campaigning, I met a grandmother from Hunterdon county. She said that society has changed dramatically from when she raised her children. She said she frequently takes care of her grandson. After reading the papers, she began to realize that she had to ask a fundamental question that she never had to ask years ago. Whenever her grandson wishes to play at another child's house she calls ahead and asks whether there is a gun in the house; if the answer is yes, she does not let her grandson go there. To often, she said, the answer is yes.

Even though New Jersey has some of the toughest gun laws in the country, the power of the gun lobby in Washington renders local efforts to control guns are meaningless. In the last two years New Jersey has witnessed not only the bloody bank robbery in Princeton, but a cop murdered in Long Branch, a deadly shooting on the NJ Turnpike, and a fifteen year old boy with a gun in school. The murder of Long Branch police Sergeant Patrick King was particularly jarring, coming just two weeks after two other policemen were shot while raiding a home in Asbury Park, New Jersey.

These violent incidents have led law enforcement

officers to reflect on the fact that violent crime has moved to the suburbs. "We have such a highly mobile society that any law enforcement agency in Monmouth County could find itself in a similar situation," John Trengrove, president of the Monmouth County Police Chiefs Association told the *Asbury Park Press*. "Years ago, people didn't move so far, but with the superhighways, a real array of all types of people come into all communities." Other law enforcement sources note an unprecedented number of chiefs of police retiring at a much younger age because the job has become extraordinarily stressful. "We're seeing a lot more guns, a lot of them carried by younger and younger people," said another suburban New Jersey law enforcement official.

America is a nation of 270 million people with 200 million guns in private ownership. About 40,000 Americans die by gunfire each year and, if current trends continue, guns will surpass motor vehicles as the leading preventable cause of death within a few years according to the National Center for Disease Control. There are roughly 12,500 handgun murders per year. Every 2 minutes somebody in the U.S. is shot. Every 14 minutes somebody dies from a gun wound. This makes the United States the most violent industrial society on earth; the chances of being killed or injured by a gun are 25 times higher than in all the European countries combined, according to the Violence Policy Center.

No citizen is immune from this scourge of violence; not Michael Jordan's father or Bill Cosby's son; not the most well compensated Chief Executive Officer or the ordinary assembly line worker.

Many common sense measures would reduce the level of gun violence and diminish the fear that our children or grandchildren will be harmed by a gun. The first step is to stop efforts to overturn the ban on assault weapons and the Brady Bill, which mandates waiting periods for gun purchasers. Extant gun control measures are under attack by the NRA and the gun manufacturers lobby, even though no serious constitutional scholar accepts the NRA's argument that the Second Amendment to the Constitution is a bar to gun control; the Supreme Court has rejected this interpretation for fifty years.

The second measure is to regulate guns the same way virtually every other consumer product is regulated in America. The Consumer Product Safety Commission has four different regulations for Teddy Bears, but none for guns. Teddy Bears are subject to four broad types of safety standards that cover sharp edges and points, small parts, hazardous materials, and flammability. Teddy Bear models are recalled as many as six times a years. Approximately one gun model is recalled every three years.

There are no requirements for the manufacture of handguns. It is easier for a child to operate a handgun than to get into a bottle of Aspirin. At a minimum, we must require trigger-locks on all guns so that it is more difficult for children to operate them; this might help reduce accidental deaths. The technology exists to personalize handguns so that only the owner can operate the gun, not a child or a criminal.

We need to increase the penalties for selling guns

to minors and increase the penalties for a minor possessing a gun. We need tougher laws to prevent criminals from getting guns. We need common sense measures that would outlaw cop-killer bullets and put a numbering system on bullets, so those bullets can be traced to a perpetrator when a gun is used for criminal purposes. There are bar codes on numerous products, like cans of soda; why not bullets? The answer is the fanatical NRA. The NRA has defeated anti-terrorism measures in the U.S. House of Representatives because the measures banned cop-killer bullets.

We also need a federal law that would limit handgun purchases to one per month per individual. This federal law would prevent individuals from driving to a state like Georgia or Florida — where there is no limit on the number of handguns that can be purchased — loading up a truck with hundreds of handguns and then re-selling those guns on a street corner to our children or to criminals.

Presently, each state has the option of setting a limit on the number of handgun purchases an individual may make in a specific time period. In New Jersey, once an individual has received a firearms identification card and a handgun purchase permit (good for the purchase of one handgun), he or she can buy up to one gun each week.

A study conducted by the Center to Prevent Handgun Violence clearly confirms that after Virginia enacted its one gun a month law in 1993, the tracing of gun's recovered in a criminal investigation to a Virginia gun dealer dropped by 57 percent for crimes committed in New Jersey. That state law has already helped save lives in New Jersey; a federal law would do even more. Even the most enthusiastic gun user does not need to purchase more than one gun a month. The NRA should stand behind this proposal because it would keep guns away from criminals. The Brady Bill was a good start. Now we need to get guns out of the hands of our children and keep New Jersey safe.

Finally, society needs to rigorously enforce the gun control laws already on the books. One such effort, called Project Exile, aims to transfer mundane arrests by local police to the federal court system where anyone caught violating even the most obscure federal gun law is zealously prosecuted. The mandatory federal sentences are much tougher than state law, and federal law can be applied not only to prosecute well-armed drug dealers, but also wife-beaters who keep a gun at home. A pilot program has succeeded in Virginia — crime is way down and drug users are rarely carrying guns. We need similar aggressive efforts here in New Jersey, and nationally.

CHAPTER SEVEN

THREE STRIKES AND YOU'RE OUT, UNLESS YOU'RE SWINGING FROM WALL STREET

*"If you do big things they print your face,
if you do little things they only print your thumbs."*
— Arthur Baer

The migration of violent gun crimes to the suburbs is not the only change in national crime patterns in the last decade. A growing incidence of white collar and financial crime affects suburban residents. Despite declining national rates in the 1990's, crime in America still remains well above the levels of the 1970's. Financial crimes that affect middle-class suburban residents, particularly the elderly, have become more prevalent.

Ironically, the "get tough on crime" and "three-strikes-and-you're-out" mentality has not been applied to financial crimes that cost the public far more than street crime. Even when prosecutors bring a case for financial crimes — which they rarely do — the prison sentences are nominal. The median jail term for fraud is just 12 months, compared to 33 months for pornography and prostitution offenses, and 60 months for drug trafficking. Even immigration violations receive 18 months. Prosecutors estimate that 90 percent of fraud offenders receive probation.

In its annual Crime in the United States Report, the FBI does not convey statistics for corporate and white collar crimes such as pollution, procurement fraud, and financial fraud. But research and anecdotal evidence suggest that crime committed by corporations continues to be an increasing problem for middle class suburban residents. The FBI reports burglary and robbery combined cost the nation $4 billion in 1995. W. Steve Albrecht, a professor of accountancy at Brigham Young estimates that white collar crime costs about fifty times as much or $200 billion annually. The FBI places the street homicide rate at around 24,000 per year. Yet, the Labor Department reports that over twice that number, 56,000, die every year from occupational diseases such as black lung, asbestosis, and occupationally induced cancer.

Many victims of white-collar crime are elderly. According to one FBI estimate, con men bilk the elderly out of $40 billion a year. The elderly are the most vulnerable because they are home at midday and available to take calls from phony tele-marketers, far and away the biggest class of crooks preying on the old. Many peddlers of phony investment schemes look for prospects by frequenting churches, country clubs, or senior citizen centers.

After expanded financial corporate criminal activity in the 1980's criminal insider trading on Wall Street and the Savings and Loan debacle — the 1990's witnessed even greater activity. Consider the following corporate crimes:

- In 1996 the nation's largest insurance company — and New Jersey political powerhouse — Prudential was fined $35 million and is paying more than $1 billion in restitution to fleeced policyholders. After an eighteen-month investigation, a task force of insurance regulators from thirty states concluded that for thirteen years Prudential salespeople used a deception called "churning," often with the knowledge and sometimes approval of officials up to at least regional vice presidents. Some unscrupulous salespeople were promoted to managerial positions because of their success at duping customers, many of them elderly and many of them living in New Jersey. "Churning" is a scam which persuaded as many as 10 million customers to use the cash value of their old insurance policies to pay the premiums on new, more expensive policies. They were not warned that the upgrading could be so costly that it would eat up their equity, leaving them with premiums they couldn't afford — and therefore no coverage. Prudential's chairman admitted that the charges were accurate and fired several salespeople and managers and a senior vice president. Some former employees became whistleblowers, providing investigators with sordid details about Prudential's operations. Employees testified that Prudential officials had ordered them to destroy any documents regarding illegal marketing practices. (Numerous insurance companies engaged in similar conduct: Mutual of New York paid $12.5 million to defrauded Alabama consumers and the *Wall Street Journal* called the settlement "the latest in a series involving alleged deceptive sales practices at many of the nation's biggest insurers.")

- The Archer Daniels Midland company, was involved in the most publicized corporate crime of recent years. Caught in a sting by Justice Department investigators, A.D.M., the world's largest grain processor, pleaded guilty to charges of conspiring to fix prices for two products: lysine, a feed supplement for livestock, and citric acid, used in soft drinks and detergents. Archer Daniels' stock price actually jumped, because Wall Street judged the settlements and fines to be bargains. In exchange for pleading guilty and promising to help the Justice Department in its expanding investigation, A.D.M. was granted immunity against charges of price-fixing in the sale of high-fructose corn syrup, which, along with the corn-derived fuel ethanol, is A.D.M.'s leading product. (ADM has a long history of contributing millions to politicians like Bob Dole. Many believe the billions of dollars of taxpayer subsidies to this industry result from these contributions.) Both taxpayers and consumers pay exorbitantly for these practices.

- According to the General Accounting Office, health care companies defraud the government out of $100 billion a year. There are reportedly 1,000 current investigations into health care fraud. Recently, SmithKline Beecham's clinical laboratory unit was allegedly close to an agreement to pay more than $300 million to the government to settle charges that it had bilked Medicare for unneeded blood tests. The record settlement is $379 million paid by National Medical Enterprises in 1994 for alleged fraud in psychiatric services.

- Military procurement fraud continues to cost taxpayers millions. The Pentagon discovered that United Telecontrol Electronics knowingly used defective bolts to hold missile launchers in place. Phony computer-controlled measurements made it look like the parts had passed inspection. Some company officials pleaded guilty to fraud; although their crime disrupted operations at air bases around the world — costing taxpayers millions — and put lives at risk, the penalties were far less severe than, say, a marijuana dealer would receive. A former U.T.E. vice president got the maximum, a light twenty-one months in prison and a $40,000 fine. According to the *Wall Street Journal*, the problem is pervasive: "In courtrooms across the country, similar scenarios are playing out. Huge and small defense contractors are facing charges of manufacturing faulty products."

Lockheed Martin, the huge military contractor, closed the longest-running influence-peddling scandal — dating back to the eighties — by paying $5.3 million on behalf of Martin Marietta Corporation, with which it merged in 1995. When such a small fine results from a $30 million overcharge, it makes business sense to continue the behavior.

McDonnell Douglas received only a $500,000 fine for misleading the Pentagon on its $6.6 billion contract to build the C-17 cargo jet. The company kept telling the government it would break even, though its own estimates showed it would lose at least $1 billion — which it did. The taxpayer paid the difference.

- Three Kentucky coal executives were sentenced to prison in the deaths of ten workers. It took seven years to convict the perpetrators. In 1989 methane gas exploded in a Pyro Mining Company shaft. Prior to the explosion the executives had lied to federal inspectors about the mine's hazardous conditions. For helping to kill ten men, the executives drew sentences ranging from five months (and a fine of $375) to eighteen months (and a $3,000 fine — or $300 per victim). The *Wall Street Journal* reported that these sentences were among the longest ever handed down. "Most criminal complaints filed on behalf of the agency result in no prison time.... The agency estimates that only about 40 people have gone to jail since 1991 because of criminal safety violations at mines."

- The minimum-wage law is frequently ignored. Princeton labor economist Alan Krueger estimates that as many as 3 million workers are paid less than the minimum wage and adds, "Violating the minimum-wage law has a certain economic logic to it because an employer, if caught, usually has to pay only the back wages that were due. Penalties are generally levied only on repeat or extreme violators." A survey of garment makers found 43 percent paying illegally low wages; trucking companies, eateries, and construction firms do the same. The Labor Department's team of inspectors has shrunk 15 percent in the past few years, and the remaining 500 inspectors are supposed to police 6 million workplaces for minimum-wage and overtime violations and child labor abuses. Workers would get an additional $19 billion a year in overtime if the rules were observed.

- The *Wall Street Journal* predicts that small-company stock manipulation may become "the dominant financial crime of the 1990s." Grand juries around the country continue to investigate this behavior. An F.B.I. sting resulted in the largest single set of arrests in securities industry history when forty-five penny-stock promoters, brokers and company officers were charged with bribery.

The elderly are particularly vulnerable to financial crime. Andrew Kandel, chief of investor protection in the New York attorney general's securities bureau, said "cold-call solicitation" of the elderly had become "pervasive in the securities industry" because the rampant bull market of the past several years has the public searching "that higher and higher return."

Even experienced and sophisticated investors can be duped by brokerage houses bent on misleading the public. Paine Webber had to pay $292 million to settle claims that its brokers had misled investors to whom they sold hundreds of millions of dollars in limited partnerships. This pales in comparison to the $1.5 billion that Prudential Securities, the brokerage arm of Prudential Insurance Company, is paying to settle charges of widespread fraud in the sale of $8 billion in limited partnerships.

Some of the most reputable firms in the country have engaged in fraudulent behavior. Take the case of Robert Farmer, the former U.S. Consul General to Bermuda. On the advice of his broker at Smith Barney, he bought $450,000 worth of shares in a biotechnology company. After losing $204,115 on the stock, Farmer discovered that his broker, who had invested heavily in the same company, was dumping his own stock at the time he was advising Farmer to buy. An arbitration panel ordered Smith Barney and the broker to pay Farmer $1 million, mostly in punitive damages. Merril Lynch was ordered by an arbitration panel to pay back almost a million dollars to an elderly couple whom the company duped into purchasing highly risky securities with the promise that their investment would be super safe.

Banks often give no more reliable advice than insurance companies or brokerage houses. A study by Prophet Market Research & Consulting found that banks do a terrible job of informing novice investors about the risks of mutual funds. An audit of 400 brokers working at banks found that one out of four didn't tell investors that mutual funds lack federal deposit insurance, and didn't mention sales charges or warn investors of possible losses.

The investing public has to be particularly cautious about the brokerage industry because it is self-policed. The self-regulatory organization is called the NASD, the National Association of Securities Dealers. As if to show that the agency is a paper tiger, it recently announced that disciplinary records of thousands of brokers had been wiped out "accidentally."

The NASD is also supposed to regulate the Nasdaq stock market — the nation's largest market for the stocks of emerging technology companies like Intel and Microsoft. But the Securities and Exchange Commission accused NASD of failing to discipline dealers who lie to customers, obscure the true value of certain stocks, and refuse to honor the prices they quote to investors. The case was settled when NASD agreed to spend $100 million over the next five years to prevent abuses on the Nasdaq market. Meanwhile, the NASD admits that the

Mafia has ties to Wall Street and nine brokerage firms and nineteen small companies are under investigation.

Even sophisticated suburban investors are vulnerable to financial crime by brokers because brokers are rarely removed from the industry. The *Wall Street Journal*, for example, found "112 individuals still active in the securities industry even though they have been on the losing side of two or more customer arbitrations from 1991 to 1995. But the industry rarely disowns a broker, and many weather grievance after grievance while continuing to earn big money selling securities. A key to survival is their ability to float from firm to firm, leaving trouble — at least temporarily — behind. One broker lost four arbitrations and had twenty-nine other customer complaints filed against him. Denied a broker's license in Ohio, he now operates in California.

The Securities Exchange Commission lacks the resources and political will to keep up with securities swindlers. The SEC doesn't even have a system for identifying and tracking of repeat offenders. As a result, serial-swindlers operate with little concern for punishment. The *Wall Street Journal* tracked the case of one career criminal, for example, who has defrauded investors for more than a quarter of a century. Despite having fleeced the public out of tens of millions of dollars, this criminal has not spent a day in jail in 20 years and still has outstanding unpaid fines and judgments of $11.5 million. This swindler is merely emblematic of a national problem. Hundreds of career swindlers go unpunished. There is a mounting inability to collect unpaid criminal debt, especially for fraud. In total, more than 100,000

Americans owe $4.5 billion in court ordered fines and restitution, a 15 fold increase from a decade ago. The SEC doesn't even know how much is owed by securities violators brought under civil law, but it believes it is in the hundreds of millions of dollars. Like the FBI, the SEC keeps no formal system for identifying or tracking repeat offenders. Apparently the fever pitch for three-strikes-and-you're-out has not spread to Wall Street.

An *Associated Press* study found that when large brokerages or their employees are caught cheating, they usually pay less in fines than firms spend on the office picnic or softball game. Typical financial penalties are only a few thousand dollars, less than a broker spends to park a car for a year in a Wall Street garage. The sweeping study of brokerage house penalties between 1980 and the mid 1990's found that fines and settlements are merely the cost of doing business and represent only 4.7 percent of total profits for the twenty largest brokerage houses in the country. Over this time period, the study found, brokerages paid only $1.37 billion in fines while earning $29 billion.

The worst violator was Prudential, the New Jersey company involved in 213 cases. Prudential, and its brokerage subsidiaries, were hit with 24 violations and paid $1.6 million in the 1980's for peddling unsuitable investments. In the 1990's, Prudential received a fine of over $1 billion for the same violation on a larger scale.

Suburban voters know that white collar and financial crime affects their pocketbook. This is particularly important given the radical changes in the way Americans save and invest. America used to be a nation of consumers and savers. Now it is a nation of investors. A person's pension is no longer guaranteed; employees are now largely on their own to make investment decisions about their retirement money. The days of savings accounts are numbered. Bank savings accounts, when adjusted for inflation, actually offer a negative rate of return. As an alternative, people invest in mutual funds. Insurance companies are no longer uniformly solid financially, so policyholders must act as investors when choosing policies. Retirees often must make investment decisions. For the first time in history, a majority of Americans now own shares in the nation's corporations. This shift from a bank/savings economy to an insurance-mutual fund/investing economy is one of the most profound in recent American economic history.

Several changes in the laws could help protect investors. Justice delayed is justice denied. It takes too long for citizens to get justice in the courts of the United States, especially when financial fraud is involved. In New Jersey's court system it often takes years for a civil case — even one involving serious injury — to reach trial. In order for investors to obtain justice, both criminal and civil procedures must be sped up. Moreover, it must be made easier for defrauded investors to recover damages in civil actions. If anything, because of profound changes in the nature of the economy in the last ten years, the legislature should consider making shareholder actions easier, not more difficult.

Second, the criminal justice system should employ creative sentencing to deter corporate criminal activity. A corporation convicted of an offense, even a misdemeanor, should be required to advertise the conviction in the largest paper or media outlet in any appropriate community. Retribution through shaming can serve an important and cost-effective deterrent function. To avoid adverse publicity, corporations will have incentive to reform their internal operations to avoid criminal activity; such a result will be achieved without the cumbersome apparatus that other criminal measures could have. The corporation is uniquely sensitive to adverse publicity, because reputation is its most prized asset. The willingness of firms to spend millions of dollars a year on "image advertising," designed to improve a corporation's profile in the eyes of the citizenry, indicates the corporation's sensitivity on this score.

By highlighting the deleterious affects of illegal activity, the corporation would be encouraged to change a corporate culture of criminal behavior. It is accepted doctrine in business school that a corporation's culture is key to financial success. And by rooting out the criminal component of a corporation's culture, the publicity sanction would serve an effective crime- fighting purpose.

Employees are only one of several corporate constituents: the community, shareholders, workers and consumers are others. A publicity sanction would simply notify the corporation's other constituents about criminal behavior. As much as employees, these constituents would help ensure that the corporation did not lapse into recidivism.

Another creative criminal legal mechanism would be suspension or, in rare cases, revocation of the charter of corporations that engage in systematic criminal behavior. The suspension of a charter can serve as a more powerful deterrent than either fines or probation. Ample precedent suggests that charter suspension or revocation can be an important regulatory tool. The SEC, for example, has the authority under the securities laws to suspend or revoke the license of a broker-dealer in securities.

Charter suspension would also become important in fighting a new class of corporate criminal: legitimate businesses controlled by organized crime. Modern organized crime increasingly manipulates the corporate form in complex ways and the mob is moving into trucking, securities and other industries that were once the preserve of legitimate business.

The doctrine of corporate criminal liability plays a particularly important role in a new, information driven economy that is witnessing novel types of crimes, often committed by organizations formed for criminal purposes. Corporate criminal liability plays a crucial role in a political order where private corporations are increasingly dominant. The Framers of the American Constitution brilliantly understood the importance of separating executive, judicial and legislative power. The Framers never anticipated, however, that a fourth branch of private economic power would come to have so much influence over the executive and legislative branches. (The Framers could not have anticipated this because at the time corporations were minor institutions, limited in scope and duration.) Permitting prosecutors to pursue corporate criminal cases serves as an important check and balance. Imposing creative sentencing mechanisms on corporations furthers this objective.

Systematic criminal activity by organizations undermines public confidence in the free enterprise system. A persistent, corrosive decline in corporate integrity has already prompted America's business leaders to rethink corporate governance; business schools nationwide have added ethics courses to the curriculum. But ethical discussions alone are insufficient. Society conveys and perpetuates its system of ethical norms through the criminal law. Only meaningful punishment for corporate criminal activity will enshrine ethical precepts.

The ends of deterrence and retribution are served by imposing corporate criminal liability and creative sentencing measures. Greater deterrence and vigilance is needed in a technological age with potentially catastrophic consequences of corporate criminal activity.

CHAPTER EIGHT

HMO'S:
HEARTLESS MONETARY ORGANS

"[U]nless the principals of the Federal Government were properly supported, and the powers of the Union increased, the honor, dignity and justice of the nation would be lost forever."
— Washington's farewell address to the Continental Army, Nov. 2, 1783, delivered at Rocky Hill, New Jersey

"The purpose of government is to provide for the people that which they can not provide for themselves."
— Abraham Lincoln

Virtually every family in America has a story about a frustrating, or worse, encounter with the health care system, usually involving an insurance company. Mine occurred when in the same year my two grandmothers — one ninety and one eighty — fell down and fractured their hips. One lives in Luxembourg, a small European nation, and one lives here. The two had identical operations to place pins in their broken bones. There the similarity ends.

My grandmother in Europe had a private room in a hospital under the single-payer system of that country — similar to those in other European countries. She also had a nurse and a physical therapist, both of whom were paid for by the government. She never touched an insurance form. My grandmother in the United States didn't have a private room and she had to pay a good portion of the costs of a nurse and a physical therapist —- even though she is fortunate enough to have private insurance, which over 40 million Americans (including many children) do not have.

She was deluged with paper. Each separate department in the hospital sent bills: the ambulance, the anesthesiologist, the surgeons, the nurses, the pharmacist. And each time, by the time she sent the bills to Medicare and to her private insurance company — which inevitably found a problem — the hospital was threatening to sue her because payment hadn't arrived from the insurance company. She didn't understand the language of co-payments, deductibles, partial fulfillments. Comparatively, she was treated well by these institutions because she is married to a doctor. I can only imagine what others go through.

I tried to take care of the matter for my grandmother but the odyssey was not resolved for a 18 months. After about seven different units of the hospital had submitted bills, I telephoned and asked: exactly how many different hospital units submit bills to patients? The verbatim response of the hospital administrator was: "I don't know; I know of at least twenty-eight billing areas, but I can't be sure." Twenty-eight billing areas? No wonder administrative costs are much higher for our insurance driven billing system than in other countries.

Every time a person goes into the hospital in this country, he or she is caught between an insurance company that wants to delay payments as long as possible and a hospital that wants to be reimbursed as soon as possible. Health Maintenance Organizations (HMOS) only exacerbate the problem.

On the campaign trail, I frequently hear from citizens frightened about the state of their health care. Like the fifty year old mother from East Brunswick, recently divorced, who was diagnosed with a pre-existing condition and as a consequence no insurance company will provide her coverage. Or the twenty-five year old man from West Long Branch who wishes to marry a co-worker at his company, but the company terminated all medical insurance benefits and he has to wonder how he and his fiancee can get these benefits. Or the woman from Princeton whose husband just changed jobs and can't get health insurance because her pregnancy is considered a "pre-existing" condition.

According to the latest federal census, in 1996 in New Jersey 1.3 million citizens had no health care coverage, including 390,000 children. Nationally, over 40 million Americans have no coverage, sixteen percent of the population. For Americans below the poverty line, over 30 percent of the population has no coverage. Although the need for a single-payer health care system is profound, the insurance and HMO lobbies in Washington have blocked any efforts at reform. The ferocious power of this lobby has been written about extensively, particularly by David Broder and Haynes Johnson in their book, *The System.* Government has made some small progress in forestalling the worst abuses of the managed care system by outlawing, for example, the requirement that mothers leave hospitals twenty four hours after giving birth. But many more incremental changes should be made until campaign finance reform and a single-payer system are achieved.

First, we need a Patients and HMO Bill of Rights that ensures that doctors, not accountants and insurance company bureaucrats, make the ultimate decisions about health care. One doctor told me how patients would come into an emergency room with head trauma in a life or death situation, and she would have to call the insurance company to receive approval before doing a CAT scan. Partly because of this, she left the practice of medicine. We also need to make sure that when a patient is hospitalized, billing disputes are resolved fairly and promptly.

Second, we need to give patients more information about doctors, hospitals, and insurance companies so they can protect themselves. Although medical malpractice is the third leading preventable cause of death in America, patients rarely know whether their doctor has erred in the past. Typically, consumers know more about who manages their retirement money or what is in their breakfast cereal than they do about their family physician. It is time to change this by posting a doctor's practice history on the Internet.

There is an urgent need for information about malpractice. A 1991 study conducted by doctors affiliated with the Harvard Medical School estimated that 180,000 Americans die every year from malpractice. That's the equivalent of three jumbo-jet crashes every two days, according to the Journal of the American Medical Association. To put this in further perspective, consider that fewer than 60,000 Americans died in the Vietnam war and that each year 45,000 people are killed in car crashes. (In a comprehensive study of New York State hospital records, the Harvard group found that 4 percent of all hospitalized patients suffered injuries resulting from medical errors that either prolonged their hospital stay or resulted in disability; fourteen percent of those injuries were fatal.)

Consumers urgently need more information to cope with a radically altered health care system that strains the venerable doctor-patient relationship. Patients rarely rely any longer on traditional sources for finding physicians, like family and friends. Instead, three-quarters of insured Americans have plans that require or give incentives to select doctors from a restricted list; increasingly, employers offer fewer plan choices and frequently change plans and doctors. Not surprisingly, a recent national opinion poll found that 75 percent of Americans think government should ensure that people have information to judge where to obtain medical care.

For government to require the electronic posting of malpractice and other information would turn the tables on a health care industry that uses extensive information about consumers to deny or limit health care coverage. Numerous states and HMOs collect and electronically store demographic, clinical and financial information; sometimes this information is sold for profit. Many HMOs — increasingly the dominant players in health care — use information about patients to avoid insuring sick or risky people to begin with.

Even more alarming for patients, the bottom-line ethos imposed by HMOs strains the doctor-patient relationship. HMOs often give doctors financial incentives to keep patients away from hospitals, from seeing specialists, and from undergoing costly tests. They give incentives to hospitals to shorten stays. When doctors owe fealty to cost-containment as well as patients, it is more important than ever for patients to be fully informed about a doctor's history, even more so for the 40 million uninsured Americans who must pay out of their own pockets for medical services.

Despite the extraordinary need for information, the medical industry has erected a veil of secrecy. A decade ago Congress created a national data bank of disciplinary actions and malpractice payments involving doctors; legislators then promptly bowed to the American Medical Association and foreclosed public access to this information. Until recently, information available from the states was not much better. In each state medical boards keep records on doctors, but information about whether doctors have been subject to malpractice proceedings is sketchy at best. Only some of these records are public and citizens must usually ask for them and then wait several weeks to see the records. Slowly, the profession's secrets are coming to light. Maryland is creating a computer bulletin board that would allow consumers to dial in and discover whether doctors have been the subject of malpractice proceedings. Massachusetts has gone even farther, creating the most detailed profiles of doctors anywhere in the county; the state plans to make them available on the Internet this spring. Three other states are also in the process of providing electronic information.

Jefferson's dictum that "information is the currency of democracy" assumes added importance in the medical arena, where the right to know can be a matter of life and death. A legitimate, limited, inexpensive role for government would be to require that a doctor's practice history be posted on the Internet, nationally and in every state. Only in this manner can we empower consumers and level the playing field as the medical profession yields to the "managed care" industry.

Third, we must protect Medicare as an important program for seniors. Before Medicare was formed in 1964, many if not most of America's elderly were getting inferior or insufficient care for illness. The advent of Medicare probably contributed more than any other single cause to the dramatic rise in the life expectancy of adult Americans during the last 30 years. No government program, with the possible exception of Social Security, has proven so cost-effective.

While Medicare has worked remarkably well for the most part, there are threats to its well-being, especially current underfunding of the trust fund and the hostility of the Republican majorities in Congress. In order to finance tax cuts, there are many proposals to raise annual premiums by $1,500 per beneficiary; to pressure senior citizens to join HMOs; and to force automatic benefit cutbacks if future costs rise faster.

The proposed herding of the elderly into managed care is especially worrisome. Recent surveys show that while most managed care beneficiaries are satisfied, a majority of those with serious health problems is anything but. HMO's attract clients by their cheap premiums but subsidize those premiums by severely rationing services, even essential ones, to the seriously ill.

The following program to defend Medicare is necessary:

1. A 5-year freeze on Medicare premiums.

2. Thereafter, premiums shall not rise faster than the consumer price index.

3. No tax reductions for the affluent at the expense of Medicare beneficiaries.

4. No rationing of Medicare services.

5. HMOs should be barred from rejecting Medicare services unless an independent panel of doctors, not financially beholden to the HMO, certifies in each individual case that a service is unimportant.

6. Funding to root out Medicare fraud and abuse should be increased. Experience with other governmental programs has shown that the incremental savings from stamping out fraud generally far exceeds the related costs of paying for the required investigations.

Fourth, we must be vigilant against attempts by insurance companies and HMOs to weaken patient and consumer protections. Many insurance companies and HMOs tried to play the role of both obstetrician and pediatrician and forced new mothers and their babies out of the hospital within 24 hours after birth. These drive-through delivery policies were dangerous because many health problems do not appear until after 24 hours and, if undetected, can lead to permanent brain damage, illness, or even death. Fortunately, New Jersey led the way in outlawing these drive-through policies. But even after it did, many companies did not comply with the law.

Another attempt by insurance companies to manipulate the system came when the industry attached an amendment to health insurance legislation in 1996 that posed a financial threat to seniors. It would have eliminated the requirement that insurance salespersons advise Medicare beneficiaries that a prospective policy duplicates their Medicare benefits. Repealing the notification requirement would have returned us to the days when American seniors were duped into purchasing unnecessary and expensive health insurance policies that provide almost no supplemental benefits. We must be ever-vigilant to oppose these type of distortions of the system.

Fifth, we have to amend the pension laws of the United States to allow for the full ability to sue if an employer denies health coverage. Right now the law is that if an employer denies health coverage — even in the case of horrific injury — an employee can sue only to have the coverage restored. Because there are no punitive damages or attorney's fees, it is hard for anyone denied medical coverage to find legal representation. Since two-thirds of all Americans have coverage through their employer, the pension laws need to be changed. These measures are all stop-gap measures until single-payer national health insurance can be passed (which will not happen until we have comprehensive campaign finance reform).

CHAPTER NINE

THE RETURN OF
THE KNOW-NOTHINGS

"I am not a Know-Nothing. As a nation we began by declaring that all men are created equal. When the Know-Nothings get control, it will read all men are created equal, except Negroes, foreigners and Catholics."
— Abraham Lincoln,
Letter to Joshua Speed. August 1855

In the summer of 1996, I attended a parade in Flemington, New Jersey commemorating the founding of the State of Israel. I found it strange that dozens of New York City Guardian Angels, the vigilante group founded by Curtis Sliwa, lined the parade route. I asked one of them to explain. He related that the parade organizers requested the help of the Guardian Angels because of death threats from a New Jersey neo-Nazi group.

Growing factions in this society reject basic premises of our history and democracy. They are extremists. Militia groups. Violent anti-choice groups. Anti-immigrant groups. Violent anti-gun control groups. There have been other periods in American history when these ideas were championed. (For example, the racist and xenophobic Know Nothing party from 1853 to 1856 fought to keep control of the government in the hands of only native born citizens). But the country has always rejected them. The alarming trend today is that certain elected officials pander to these groups and even espouse their ideology of intolerance.

These extremists have made such inroads that even a moderate suburban district like Central New Jersey has neo-Nazi groups and the elected Representative espouses radical right-wing views. If this type of extremism takes hold here, it can take hold anywhere. Consider, for example, a description in the *Asbury Park Press* of the views of the Representative from Central New Jersey:

"Thomas L. Vivian arrives at the Spinning Wheel Diner with a menu of his own. On an index card, he has listed a political agenda he wants to share with his representative in Washington. The list reads like a declaration of conservative dogma."

"Quit the United Nations, which is usurping national sovereignty and 'moving toward a world government.' Increase defense spending. Resume civil defense preparedness. Abolish the National Endowment for the Arts. Shut down the Department of Education. Stop judges from making laws. End the 'abortion of children'..."

"As for his new representative? Vivian listened intently as he addressed his questions and those of several other patrons inside the Lebanon diner on a recent Saturday morning. "Later he delivered his verdict: 'So far, so good.' Constituents like Vivian bring out the deeply conservative side of Central New Jersey's newest congressman."

"With $7,295 in donations, the Republican National Coalition for Life was his leading campaign contributor, according to the Center for Responsive Politics. Another major donor was the National Rifle Association, which gave $3,000. His campaign chairman is Dale Florio, the chief lobbyist for tobacco interests in Trenton."

"He was one of only three New Jersey House members who voted to dismantle the National Endowment for the Arts. All five Democrats in the state's delegation, and four of the seven Republicans, voted against the measure 'Regarding abortion, my position is very clear on that. I support the right to life. I think that's rooted in our consti-

tution. And through the court system . . . the life of the unborn, the life of human beings, has been denigrated.'"

Forget the fact that nobody, except this Congressman, believes that the Framers of the United States Constitution intended to protect the rights of fetuses. Even more incredibly, this Congressman is on record as supporting an Amendment to the Constitution that would protect the life of the unborn. Yet, he just said the Constitution already protects the life of the unborn! Why amend the Constitution to do something it already does?

The larger point is that these irresponsible views, increasingly represented in New Jersey and in the Congress, must be opposed. Many extremists in Congress want to repeal the federal ban on assault weapons. One Representative from upstate New York, Gerald Solomon, fervently argues for a repeal of the ban because his wife, who lives in upstate New York, needs to have an Uzi to protect herself.

Congresswoman Helen Chenowith from Idaho believes that the UN is flying "black helicopters" over militia compounds in the Northwest in preparation for a UN invasion. Former Congressman Bob Dornan used to rant on the House floor about "homos" and a "disloyal, betraying little Jew." Dornan once called a fellow congressman a "draft dodging wimp" and a "liar." While running for re-election, Dornan said: "Every lesbian spearchucker in this country is hoping I get defeated." (Dornan is running again for the House.)

These views are irresponsible, intolerant, fanatical and contrary to the traditions of the country. We must oppose politicians who appeal to these elements and support politicians who favor tolerance and an open discussion of ideas.

Today, we see extremist ideas gaining currency — thwarting more meaningful controls on guns and severely compromising a women's right to choose. Congress has enacted a ban on abortions on military bases, even if paid for by private insurance. Roughly sixty percent of counties in the United States do not have a clinic that can perform an abortion procedure for women, because the clinics have either been intimidated or forced to close because of discriminatory government regulations passed specifically to shut them down. The twenty fifth anniversary of *Roe v. Wade* has seen another wave of bombings at clinics across the county; and when a national newspaper did an article reproductive choice, not one doctor would be quoted by name or photographed for fear of violent reprisal. Supporters of extremist politicians distribute leaflets of dead fetuses in New Jersey churches and accuse Republican supporters of abortion rights of being murderers. A majority of Republican Senators back a right to life amendment that would have the United States government prosecute doctors for murder.

Many elected officials want to enact mandatory prayer in school, even though this is contrary to separation of Church and State and a renunciation of the ideals of the signers of the Mayflower compact. Extremists would have us believe that nearly all religious expression and activities are banned in our nation's public schools.

In fact, private religious expression in the public schools is almost always protected, while any school endorsement of religion is always prohibited. We must continue to support a strict interpretation of the Establishment Clause of the First Amendment which separates church and state. History demonstrates that the ineluctable result of a union of government and religion is the destruction of freedom for those with minority views.

This is why the United States Supreme Court has clearly ruled that organized vocal prayer and ceremonial reading from the Bible are unconstitutional practices in the public school classroom; nor is organized prayer permitted at student assemblies, athletic activities and special events. Our current constitutional scheme leaves plenty of room for students to engage in non-coercive individual prayer that does not substantially disrupt the school's educational mission and activities. For example, all students have the right silently to say a prayer before a test or grace before a meal. But school officials must not be involved with prayer in any way, since any school promotion or endorsement of a religious activity is unconstitutional.

Those that want to enact a compulsory prayer in school are trying to place their religious views before those of others. These same extremists obscure the fact that students have a constitutionally protected right to pray privately and even to distribute religious materials.

We must be vigilant in ensuring that extreme factions are not allowed to impede vibrant democratic debate, either in New Jersey or nationally.

CHAPTER TEN

ONLY THE LITTLE PEOPLE PAY TAXES (WITH APOLOGIES TO LEONA HELMSLEY)

"A penny saved is a penny earned."
— Ben Franklin, Poor Richard's Almanac

My grandmother set a family example of thriftiness. Decades after World War II we would go shopping and she would still place discarded pieces of vegetable into her pocketbook and bring them home to make soup. She always had in mind the memory of lacking food during the War.

In my first political job, working for Ralph Nader, I learned from one of America's great penny-pinchers. Ralph was legendary for walking into the office late at night and weighing pieces of mail on a postal scale to determine if the staff had used too much postage. Nader continues to practice what he preaches, and his crusades to stop governmental and corporate waste will set examples for future generations.

While working with Nader, I was fortunate enough to co-author a book, published by Sierra Club Press, that investigated how taxpayers can earn a greater return from the assets they own: the timber, minerals and other resources located on the public lands of the United States. The law permits corporations, including many foreign companies, to take for free billions of dollars of gold, silver and other minerals that are owned by the taxpayers of the United States. The book suggested ways to stop this practice.

As a consumer advocate and lawyer I have tried to fight for taxpayers, consumers, and ratepayers and against wasteful spending and collusive pricing. I continued my taxpayer advocacy as an elected official in Princeton. The budgets I voted for contained the lowest tax increases in twelve years and devised innovative programs for saving taxpayer dollars. I proposed a Taxpayers Bill of Rights for local taxpayers.

The first plank in this Bill of Rights is a readily understandable and user-friendly property tax bill. Prior to my election, the annual bill presented to taxpayers in the Township was hardly a model of clarity. Indeed, if a bill were submitted to a customer in any other context, the customer would send the bill back to the vendor for clarification. Even local utility bills — prepared by large monopolies — give far more information than Princeton's tax bills. Ironically, for most taxpayers the largest check they write during the course of the year — other than one to the IRS — is for their property tax bill. Princeton property tax bills historically neglected a number of important variables. Have taxes risen faster than the rate of inflation? Can't tell. Where exactly do our taxes go, and at what percentage? Can't tell. Are the budgets of the government entities that use our taxes — the School Board, the township, and County Government — rising faster than the rate of inflation? Can't tell.

It is the obligation of Government to treat taxpayers as valued customers, not automatic check-writers. The new tax bill would give tables and charts that compare each taxpayer's bill to the preceding five year period. I proposed that each bill have the following components: comparisons to the rate of inflation; comparisons to other municipal tax rates in this County; and comparisons to other municipal tax rates with comparable socio-economic profiles in New Jersey. Also, each bill should contain a toll-free number that taxpayers can call to find out 1) how to appeal their property tax assessments; 2) how to readily obtain a clear copy of the Township and other relevant budgets; and 3) how to obtain any further information.

My local Taxpayers Bill of Rights was based on conversations with taxpayers and homeowners I have met in Princeton while campaigning door-to-door. The appropriate slogan might be: "No taxation without clear presentation." Although many of the items in my Taxpayer Bill of Rights were not passed by the local elected council, some were and tax bills were made more clear as a result.

I opposed wasteful spending on boondoggles like a $9 million municipal building and enacted other reforms that help taxpayers. For example, after reviewing Princeton's budget I determined that one out of every twenty dollars was spent on insurance. I immediately requested an audit and eventually we reduced our bills by several hundred thousand dollars because we found more competitive carriers.

I also publicly raised the issue of the disastrous tax consequences of building an incinerator in Mercer County. County taxes are the second largest component of the property tax bill (after education) and they have been rising faster than the rate of inflation. I went to the hearings on the incinerator, exposed the flawed economics, and the wasteful spending, and stood up for the taxpayer. (Whatever one thinks of the environmental effects of incinerators, the County was wasting money by writing no-bid contracts and spending millions on expensive studies and consultants.)

Sometimes creativity is the key to saving taxpayer dollars. During my tenure, Princeton had the opportunity to purchase a large parcel of land and preserve it as Open Space. Open Space is the best deal the taxpayer can get because it ensures that the land does not fall in the hands of a developer who will develop the property and increase education, sewer, and road costs.

Another idea, to save money for the taxpayer was to write a letter to all the neighbors of the parcel that Princeton planned to purchase, asking them to contribute to the acquisition of the Open Space land. The theory was that each neighbor benefits from the land being permanently placed in Open Space. Nobody believed that the neighbors would voluntarily contribute, but the week after we sent the letters, a foundation that owned land adjacent to the proposed Open Space parcel sent in a check for more than $100,000. Soon other neighbors chipped in and in the end we saved the taxpayers a significant amount of the purchase price. This idea of leveraging Open Space acquisitions can be used at any level of government.

As a local elected official, I also tried to re-write the bargain with real estate developers so they pay the cost of expanded sewer, road and education costs rather than sticking the taxpayer with these costs. I proposed more aggressively pursuing commercial developers that are delinquent in tax payments and allowing citizens to decide in a referendum which major building projects to support and which to reject. I also suggested revising the collection of taxes. There is automatic billing for everything else in this country, and even the IRS allows electronic filing of returns. I recommended that Princeton devise a system permitting property taxes to be paid by credit card, or debited electronically; other jurisdictions have had success with this approach, and it has led to lower costs. Finally, I was able to convince Princeton's governing body to offer a reward for ideas from Princeton residents that save taxpayers money. The best ideas come from the people.

While working for taxpayer rights on a local level, I also opposed a disturbing tax trend that exists at every level of government — radically increased user fees that amount to regressive taxes. Consider some examples in New Jersey in the past few years:

- increased from $2 to $5 dollars the co-payment for Pharmaceutical Assistance for the Aged and Disabled. This is an increase of 150 percent.

- the state has imposed fees for taking a civil service test and for filing civil-rights complaints.

- the state increased the fee for filing for divorce from $25 to $160.

- increased the fee for hospital admissions to $5, from $4.55.

Perhaps the most insulting user fee the State of New Jersey ever passed is the fee requiring citizens to pay for information supplied by the State. If information is the currency of democracy, this state is bankrupt. The notion that taxpayers have to pay in advance, in exact change, for information that should be free in a democracy is astounding. It's bad enough that taxpayers pay for this information when we fund our government officials, but to have to pay for it twice is an insult.

For another insult, consider that New Jersey taxpayers pick up the tab for junkets to New Jersey casinos and other locales not once, but four times. Taxpayers pay once because local tax dollars fund politicians who frolic in the casinos with, say, the League of Municipalities. Most municipalities reimburse local officials who attend the Atlantic City event. At 14,000 attendees, with an average bill of almost $500, this is a $7 million subsidy coming directly from property taxes — to Donald Trump and the other casino owners.

New Jersey taxpayers pay a second and third time, because the businesses that sponsor junkets at the Atlantic City casinos and elsewhere write-off the expense on their corporate income taxes for both federal and state tax purposes. When companies deduct the junkets, the taxpayer bears a greater tax burden.

The taxpayer pays a fourth time because these junkets offer corporate interests an opportunity to extract special favors and tax breaks from elected officials. Can I prove that the reason real estate developers ply politicians with gifts, junkets, and campaign contributions is to extract favorable treatment by local zoning boards and municipal planners? No. Am I sure that it happens? Yes. Common sense points in this direction. The corporate lobbyists have the motive and the opportunity to unduly influence legislators. And the result is unplanned, unchecked growth in the most crowded state in the nation, resulting in severe traffic problems. The taxpayer picks up the costs of overcrowding, extra sewage, over-burdened schools etc. Can I prove that the electric utility monopoly PSE&G's lavish event at Atlantic City is designed to influence local officials to prevent the dereg-ulation of energy prices resulting in millions of dollars of savings to taxpayers? No. Am I sure this is the motive and result? Yes.

Because the political process is gamed by the lob-byists, the rates for water, electricity, insurance and a host of other goods and services rise much faster than the rate of inflation. I was honored to have the opportu-nity to fight for lower cable, water, electric utility and tax rates. But no matter what reforms are passed on a local or state level, tax policy is driven by Washington. Washington has not been kind to individual taxpayers, but the corporations are laughing all the way to the bank.

Over the last twenty years Congress has shifted programs and services from the federal government to local and state governments, but not the money to pay for them. While the federal government pretends to cut taxes or spending, the net effect is simply to shift the burden to the homeowner.

Nationally, local real estate tax collections between 1980 and 1991 spiraled from $66 billion to $162 billion — an increase of 145 percent — the highest rate of increase of any tax in the nation. In 1950 all local and state tax collections amounted to 45 percent of federal tax collections. By 1991, that figure had surged to 82 percent. If current trends continue, real estate taxes will surpass federal income taxes as the largest tax source of revenue by the year 2000.

The major reason for the crushing burden on middle-class taxpayers in this country, however, is the special favors for corporations that politicians write into the tax code. Taxes are only for the little people and the unincorporated.

Every April 15, while millions of Americans struggle with Byzantine forms and rising tax rates, the chieftains of America's largest corporations celebrate an increasingly benevolent Tax Code. The tax burden on corporations, particularly large corporations, is declining while it gets tougher for average American families to meet their tax obligations every year. Individuals pay up to 40 percent of their income to the federal government. Combined with rising local and state taxes, many citizens will fork over 50 percent of their income to the government. This estimate does not even include user fees: the hidden taxes politicians have been quietly hiking for the last decade. When taxpayers renew their driver's license, or obtain a marriage certificate, or use emergency medical services, they are paying tariffs that have far outpaced the inflation rate in recent years. Corporations, by contrast, pay at most 35 percent of their income in federal taxes, making American corporate tax rates among the lowest in the western industrial world. (Many European nations impose a 40 percent corporate tax rate, while Germany, for example, taxes corporations at a 50 percent rate.)

In practice, corporations almost never pay the full tax rate because of plentiful loopholes unavailable to individuals. Companies can deduct rent, repairs, and other expenses, can reincorporate or move overseas to escape tax liability, and can hide assets. (It is well documented that multinational corporations frequently underreport the amount of income earned in the United States.) The non-partisan Tax Foundation, a Washington research group, estimates that when all deductions and loopholes are accounted for, the effective federal corporate income tax rate is only 23 percent. And the percentage of federal receipts attributable to corporate taxes has fallen dramatically since the 1970's (from a high of 17 percent in 1970 to only around 10 percent today).

Individuals increasingly bear the burden of federal, state and local taxation because special interest lobbyists have jerry-rigged the entire structure to benefit large corporations. These lobbyists swarm Capitol Hill daily, ramming through special tax treatment for cigarette advertising, savings and loan operators, and agribusiness. Each loophole adds another layer of complexity. This intricacy, while benefitting Big Business, has turned the Tax Code into what President Bush's Tax Commissioner called "a virtually impenetrable maze" for individuals. Congress has compounded the problem by enacting eleven major revisions to the Tax Code since 1981, further diminishing respect for the system and undermining the willingness of even law-abiding taxpayers to calculate their tax burden properly.

When Jimmy Carter called the Tax Code "a disgrace to the human race," he didn't realize that corporate loopholes would be expanded and extended. An illuminating example is the $3 billion a year tax break for corporations that operate in the United States Commonwealth of Puerto Rico. This one provision of the Tax Code, Section 936, allows corporations to take a tax credit for the amount of profit they make in Puerto Rico. Giant American pharmaceutical corporations are the principal beneficiaries of this largesse. The General Accounting Office, the investigative arm of Congress, found that the tax savings of one concern, Pfizer, amounts to about $156,000 per worker or six times the average compensation for workers at Pfizer's Puerto Rican operations. Sadly, this tax dodge, while draining the Treasury, is in no way linked to the number of jobs corporations create for the depressed Puerto Rican economy.

The Great Corporate Tax Loophole Machine just keeps on rolling under an Administration allegedly committed, in the words of President Clinton, to "breaking the stranglehold ... the lobbyists have on our government." After a multi-year, multi-million dollar lobbying effort, the drug industry convinced the Clinton Administration to retain the preponderance of the Puerto Rican subsidy. No resources were spared in the effort to rescue a corporate tax subsidy: lobbying firms, law firms, former members of Congress and other wheeler-dealers were all enlisted. And Section 936 is only one example: the Office of Management and Budget estimates that in 1994 taxpayers will lose $53.3 billion in various tax breaks for corporations.

Despite promises of tax reform from politicians, the so-called "Tax Freedom" day for individuals keeps moving back. This means that if the average middle income tax-payer's 1997 salary, starting from January 1, went only to pay taxes, it would have taken until May 3 for that tax-payer to make all payments. By comparison, this Tax Freedom day was March 8 in 1940, and would have been sometime in April before the 1980's.

Another massive inequity in the federal (and state) tax code is the greater ability of corporations to take deductions. If a citizen is sued and has to pay a judgment, he or she cannot deduct that judgment. But if a corporation has to pay a judgment, the company not only may take a write-off, but might get a check from Uncle Sam to offset past earnings. Some prominent examples:

- Exxon took a $1.9 billion write-off in spilling millions of gallons of crude oil into Prince William Sound.

- The Wall Street brokerage firm Salomon Brothers settled charges of skimming millions of dollars from the federal government and deducted the $290 million settlement.

- Dow Corning can deduct from its tax bill the billions it must pay out to victims of its silicone breast implants.

- Bankers Trust can subtract from its tax bill the millions it paid to settle suits over its money losing derivative products.

While Congress has cut Medicare, Medicaid and other

social welfare programs, the favorable tax treatment of corporations continues unabated, consider:

- Export incentives worth $7 billion a year are a waste of money because companies will naturally try to sell overseas.

- Nearly 60 percent of US controlled corporations and 74 percent of foreign firms doing business here paid no federal tax in the last year for which figures were available.

- Most tax breaks go to already prosperous industries. For example, the oil and energy industry receives $2.4 billion each year while $1.4 billion go to timber and natural resource companies. Billions more go to insurance, agriculture, real estate, and other concerns.

The tax system reflects the increasing power of the corporate lobby. After World War II, the nation's tax bill was shouldered about equally between corporations and individuals. But after decades of loopholes, the corporate share of the burden has declined to about one fourth of what individuals pay. (A similar trend has emerged concerning state tax revenue.)

Business prefers tax breaks because, unlike spending programs, they are outside the federal budget and not subject to annual congressional review. Not surprisingly, between 1913 and 1986, Congress killed only 13 of the scores of tax breaks on the books, according to the General Accounting Office.

There are numerous areas for reform. The government should crack down on foreign corporations that do not pay taxes in the United States. The General Accounting Office estimates that these companies evade hundreds of millions of dollars a year in federal taxes. The nation will lose $70 billion to $100 billion over the next seven years because the largest and most profitable foreign corporations that operate in the United States will pay no taxes. (The GAO concluded that over 25,000 foreign-bases multinational firms operating in the U.S. paid no income tax despite sales of over $400 billion.)

Government also needs to eliminate the hundreds of loopholes and deductions that make the 1040 form so complicated that a majority of Americans have to hire an accountant just to complete their tax returns.

As they spend more time and money each year on tax compliance, citizens may want to consider demanding that when politicians enact tax laws, at the federal, state and local level, they stop coddling the special corporate interests and start elevating the concerns of individuals.

CHAPTER ELEVEN

DONALD TRUMP
NEEDS A HANDOUT?

"A government that robs Peter to pay Paul can always count upon the support of Paul."
— George Bernard Shaw

I participate in "Operation Santa Claus." This model federal program, which costs the taxpayer nothing, was started by employees of the U.S. Post Office who wanted to make a difference. Needy children from around the country write to "Santa Claus." The letters are deposited at the Central Post Office in New York City and volunteers like myself act as "Santa Claus" by answering requests.

I responded to a letter dated December 15, 1996, from a twelve year old New Jersey boy from Camden:

Dear Santa Claus:

Hi. I'm writing to you because I need your help Santa because my mom can't go to buy us anything because she just came out of the hospital because she had HIV and she gets lots of colds. I'm writing to you because my father passed away and we don't have any money to buy any gifts because of the funeral expenses. My mom can not buy us anything. Soon we will not have a father or a mother. Santa, can you help us please?

Lewis R.

As I sent gifts to Lewis and his family, I reflected on the state of welfare in New Jersey and in the nation. Twenty percent of American children live below the poverty line as defined by the federal government, a much higher percentage than in any other advanced industrial country. Thousands of children like Lewis live in searing poverty in New Jersey. With its seventy percent dropout rate, rising unemployment, and Third-World caliber infant mortality rate, Camden is the poorest city of its size in the nation.

Assume those that want to deny welfare to Lewis are right. If so, society must also terminate welfare benefits for the privileged. If you cut welfare for Lewis, you ought to cut it for Donald Trump. Only a society with twisted priorities could ignore the plight of Lewis and lavish payments on billionaires from Nevada and New York. Incredibly, as welfare for Lewis becomes more scarce, welfare for out-of-state casino moguls becomes more generous.

Consider the deal struck with the State of New Jersey by Steve Wynn, the Nevada billionaire and owner of Mirage resorts. New Jersey Governor Whitman agreed in 1997 that the state and other government sources (read: the taxpayer) would pay the lion's share of the estimated $ 330 million cost of building a 1.6-mile road-tunnel from the end of the Atlantic City Expressway to the Marina District of Atlantic City where Wynn wants to construct a $ 1.85 billion casino complex. The government also let Wynn's company, Mirage Resorts Inc., off the hook for any cost overruns and agreed to pick up the entire tab should the casino project be terminated. In addition to the road-tunnel Wynn demanded, the Whitman administration agreed to reimburse Mirage, through a sales tax break, for 75 percent ($ 26 to $ 27 million) of the $35 million cost of cleaning up the landfill on which the casino complex is to be built. And all this comes on top of Atlantic City giving Wynn the approximately 150-acre site for $1. As one New Jersey newspaper put it: "If ever there was corporate welfare, this is it." And Wynn does not need the welfare because his four Nevada casinos gross nearly a billion per year! (The only controversy this deal generated was from Wynn rival Donald Trump, a New York billionaire who himself has been the recipient of plenty of New Jersey style corporate largesse.)

The Atlantic City tunnel deal is only the tip of the iceberg when it comes to corporate welfare in New Jersey. Consider some other recent examples:

- A measure that sets aside $75 million collected by the Casino Reinvestment Development Authority for the construction of new hotel rooms. This money was supposed to go to improve the community, not subsidize the very casinos obligated under law to contribute to community development.

- Hanjin, South Korea's biggest cargo line, with revenues approaching $3 billion, received a five-year, 50 percent grant returning half of the payroll's state income taxes to the company.

- MSNBC, a subsidiary of General Electric Company, the largest firm in the world, was given an 80 percent rebate on payroll taxes for 10 years.

- Anadigics Inc. of Warren Township was also given a 10-year, 80 percent payroll tax break.

- The electric utilities are asking the state to have ratepayers and taxpayers pay for the cost of nuclear power plants that don't work. These "stranded costs" are estimated at $7 to 17 billion, or $1,000 to 2,500 for every state resident. Consumers and taxpayers are being asked to pay for PSE&G's Hope Creek nuclear plant. Built at a cost of $4.5 billion, this nuclear plant was 12 years behind schedule and 2,000 percent over budget. PSE&G's two Salem nuclear plants have not produced a watt of power in two years, yet consumers continue to pay over $200 million per year in electric rates for these plants. There has never been a systematic study of the costs of corporate welfare programs in New Jersey. There needs to be. The citizens of New Jersey should also have initiative and referendum to vote on these corporate welfare projects. If put to a vote of the people, these welfare payments would have been stopped a long time ago.

There have, however, been several comprehensive studies of corporate welfare programs at the federal level. Thinkers and leaders from across the political spectrum agree that the federal government spends up to $167 billion every year on corporate welfare packages that need to be eliminated. Consider some examples:

- $1.6 million in federal funds for McDonald's, partly to help market Chicken McNuggets in Singapore from 1986 to 1994.

- $20,000 for golf balls that defense manufacturer Lockheed- Martin billed the federal government as an "entertainment expense."

- $300,000 to improve fireworks at Disney theme parks.

- $278 million in technology subsidies to Amoco, Citicorp, General Motors, and IBM.

- $100 million annually to Gallo, McDonald's, Ocean Spray and other food companies for international advertising.

- When Saudi Arabia took bids for its new phone system, the White House picked up the phone and urged the Saudi government to accept the bid of AT&T, despite the fact that AT&T's bid was not the lowest.

- The United States has created a fund to bail out the nuclear programs of the former Eastern bloc. This fund will benefit huge American corporations.

- $1.4 billion in sugar subsidies that go to the largest 1 percent of sugar farms.

- $99 million that the U.S. Forest Service pays each year to build logging roads in national forests. The service has built 340,000 miles of road or eight times the length of the interstate highway system, for the benefit of the logging companies.

These examples don't begin to cover the $167 billion in subsidies to mining companies and timber companies or the synfuel tax credits, nuclear subsidies, agribusiness subsidies, insurance loopholes, and taxpayer funding of the Savings and Loan bailout. Most of these corporate welfare programs benefit large corporations, many foreign. According to the former Secretary of Labor, these corporations have not created, one net new job from 1975 to the mid-1990's. The small corporations that are the dynamic job creators in the economy do not get these breaks. Congress, hypocritically, has found a trillion dollars in cuts in the last several years, the bulk of it from social services to the poor, while less than two percent of those cuts came from subsidies to industry.

Many of the subsidies seem correlated to government contributions. The sugar industry gave $5.5 million to federal campaigns in the last few years and manages to consistently kill attacks on price supports. ADM, which controls 80 percent of the ethanol industry, prevented the elimination of ethanol subsidies which would have cost $3.6 billion over five years. The company gave almost $500,000 to Democrats and $400,000 to Republicans in recent election cycles. Perhaps the biggest proposed welfare program is the call to have $400 billion in Social Security taxes collected each year invested in the stock market. This would be the biggest subsidy of Wall Street brokerage houses ever. The fact that government entities like Orange County California or West Virginia lost millions investing in the market should make us thing twice about leaving the retirement savings of millions of investors to the brokerage houses.

The fact that government increasingly responds to corporations' requests for welfare reflects the growing power of multinational companies relative to governments. Of the 100 largest economies in the world, 51 are corporations; only 49 are countries. Wal-Mart, the No.12

company, is bigger than 161 countries including Israel, Poland and Greece. The combined sales of the world's top 200 companies is far greater than a quarter of the world's economic activity. General Motors' sales are larger than the gross national product of Denmark.

Increasingly, these multinational companies demand not just national, but also international welfare and subsidies. Often, these demands take the form of trade agreements with favorable terms for multinationals. The trade agreements signed by the United States in recent years permit the importation of goods made by child labor. Providing access to cheap labor unavailable in the United States is a form of subsidy.

New Jersey was once a leader in the nation's battle to end the tragic scourge of child labor. In 1916 New Jersey governor Woodrow Wilson signed into law an act regulating the use of child labor in industry. Although the measure was later declared unconstitutional by the Supreme Court, the United States forever banned the use of child labor with the enactment of the 1938 Fair Labor Standards Act. Ironically, many products that we use and purchase in our New Jersey communities today are manufactured abroad using child labor — products ranging from soccer balls to rugs to clothing to toys. These goods are permitted in the country under a variety of trade deals that the United States has signed over the years. Approximately 120 million of the world's children under the age of 14 labor full-time, according to the International Labor Organization. (If those for whom work is a secondary activity are included, the number rises to 250 million). Consider their plight:

- Children in the Asian rug industry often toil in cramped quarters, hovering over their work in poorly lit rooms; they often develop spinal deformities from persistent crouching and respiratory ailments from chronic exposure to rug byproducts in poorly ventilated quarters.

- In Pakistan, the world's leading exporter of soccer balls (supplying more than 60 percent of the U.S. market), more than 7,000 children under the age of 14 toil at stitching the balls. They receive about 60 cents per ball, and even older children can only stitch three or four balls a day.

- In Columbia, hundreds of children are used to mine coal.

Corporations have benefitted enormously from the trade agreements signed by the United States government in recent years. GATT, NAFTA and several similar initiatives have all offered benefits to companies not only by allowing the use of child labor, but by lowering environmental, health and safety and other standards. Welfare for multinational companies, however, has not benefitted the country. The North American Free Trade Agreement (NAFTA), in operation for almost four years, is costing jobs, hurting the environment, and lowering the standard of living for the people of North America. NAFTA has weakened border inspections to check for contaminated food, illegal drugs, and dangerous trucks. As a result, more unsafe food is reaching our supermarkets, more illegal drugs are invading our communities and more hazardous trucks are driving on U.S. highways. The hidden effects on New Jersey citizens' daily lives are enormous:

- Multinational corporations have the right under NAFTA to file special court challenges to overturn environmental laws that get in the way of trade profits. NAFTA, thus gives a Mexican or Canadian corporation the right to come into a small town anywhere in the U.S. and file suit to overturn clean-air, clean-water, or other environmental regulations. In fact, that frightening scenario is already a reality. The Ethyl Corporation of Virginia has filed a $250 million lawsuit against the Canadian government, under NAFTA rules, after Canada banned a toxic gasoline additive. If Ethyl wins its case, governments will have to pay polluters not to pollute.

- Food-related illness in the U.S. is on the rise: dangerous beef, contaminated strawberries, raspberries and basil. Increasingly, these threats involve imported food. The United States is importing an increasingly larger share of its food supply. But recent international trade agreements, such as NAFTA and the Uruguay Round of the General Agreement on Tariffs and Trade (GATT), restrict how food safety can be protected in the United States. Today's trade rules determine a nation's ability to set pesticide contamination limits, beef inspection standards, and what chemicals or other additives are allowed. Consider:

- Under NAFTA, food imports from Mexico and Canada have dramatically increased (40 percent), while inspection of foods imported from Mexico and

Canada has decreased. Food from Mexico is more likely to be contaminated with illegal levels of pesticides than U.S. grown food. Beef produced in Canada, which has increased under NAFTA, is not properly inspected at the U.S. border.

- The increased volume of trade under NAFTA has undermined the ability of the U.S. to protect U.S. farmers against pests and disease, jeopardizing U.S. grown food. Meat and poultry imported from Mexico and Canada are not inspected for dangerous chemicals which may be used in those countries.

Multinational companies want even more international corporate welfare programs, and the President wants Congress to give him "fast track" authority to rapidly expand failed trade agreements with other nations. Under a "fast track" law, Congress can't fully debate or amend any trade agreements that the White House negotiates. All Congress gets to do is vote a simple "yes" or "no." The result will be to diminish environmental and food safety standards further. The vast majority of Americans oppose fast track authority and these trade deals. Whether it is corporate welfare at the local and state level, or international trade deals signed in Washington, the largesse shown to powerful companies affects the lives of New Jersey residents. Only by curbing the power of these corporate lobbies can we genuinely reform the welfare system.

CHAPTER TWELVE

JOE CAMEL LOVES NEW JERSEY

"The cops reported you as just another homicide.
But I can tell that you were just frustrated
From living with Murder Incorporated."
— Bruce Springsteen

After spending over $100 million on a lobbying campaign to kill congressional oversight, the cigarette industry is riding tall in the saddle. There is no more shameless lobby in the country — the industry's claims have gone from brazen to incredible to farcical. No matter how fatuous the arguments, New Jersey has a love affair with Big Tobacco.

Big Tobacco still says there is no scientific evidence that tobacco is harmful to human health, and denies that the industry markets to children or "spikes" its product for an added nicotine kick. The twisted mental gymnastics that support these claims make for real comedy. In Richard Kluger's Pulitzer prize winning account of the American tobacco industry, he recalled an interview with Helmut Wakeham, chief scientist for Philip Morris.

Wakeham: None of the things which have been found in tobacco smoke are in concentrations which should be considered harmful.

Interviewer: But the components themselves can be considered harmful, can they not?

Mr. Wakeham: Anything can be considered harmful. Applesauce is harmful if you get too much of it.

Interviewer: I do not think many people are dying from applesauce.

Mr. Wakeham: They are not eating much.

Interviewer: People are smoking a lot of cigarettes.

Mr. Wakeham: Well, let me say it this way. The people who eat applesauce are dying. The people who eat sugar die. The people who smoke die. Does the fact that the people who smoke cigarettes die demonstrate that smoking is the cause?

This interview was in 1976. By 1997, the tobacco industry still had not changed its tune. As *New York Times* columnist Bob Herbert recalls, the president of R.J. Reynolds, Andrew Schindler, testified under oath that he doesn't believe tobacco has been linked to any illness and he doesn't think it is any more addictive than carrots.

"Carrot addiction?" asked a lawyer.

"Yes," replied Mr. Schindler. "There was British research on carrots."

How could anyone believe the industry markets to children? Just because Joe Camel is as recognizable to youngsters as Mickey Mouse? Could children possibly be enticed by the RJ Reynolds cigarette called "Jumbos" which has an elephant on the front and back of the box. (Also on the box is a little man in the moon blowing smoke rings; on each cigarette is a little picture of an elephant.)

The fact is that tobacco companies studied teenagers' smoking habits for decades and tried to develop cigarettes that youths would find alluring. In February 1973 RJ Reynolds' Claude Tague Jr., a top company scientist, wrote a twelve page research memo titled: "Some Thoughts About New Brands of Cigarettes for the Youth Market"; it describes the desired tar and nicotine levels for a cigarette aimed at first time users or "learners." The memo says Reynolds could pursue smokers under age 21 since there is "nothing immoral or unethical about our company attempting to attract those smokers to our product."

Studies show that kids 16-25 are far more likely to switch brands than older adults, which is why the company targeted this group. A 1992 survey of elementary and middle school students by Bedford Kent Group for RJR shows that while only 4 percent of them had tried smoking, 90 percent could identify Camel as a brand of cigarette and 73 percent could identify Marlboro. RJR and BAT Industries studied young smokers and their habits in an effort to woo them to their brands. Part of the effort included suggesting the companies engineer the nicotine and tar yields of cigarettes to affect the density of smoke, the taste of the smoke, and the overall appeal to "learners."

In 1990 an RJR division manager in Sarasota, Florida wrote to company sales representatives asking them to identify stores close to high schools and colleges. "The purpose is to identify those stores during 1990 where we would try to keep premium items [cigarettes for teenagers] in stores at all times," said a Jan. 10, 1990 memo from the manager.

Documents uncovered in litigation are more and more embarrassing to the tobacco companies. A 1975 RJ Reynolds memorandum opined: "To ensure increased and longer term growth for Camel filter, the brand must increase its share penetration among the 14 to 24 age group, which have a new set of more liberal values and which represent tomorrow's cigarette business." In 1972 Brown & Williamson Tobacco Corporation came up with a scheme to add sweet flavors like Coca-Cola or apple to its cigarettes. "It's a well known fact that teenagers like sweet products," reads a company memo. "Honey might be considered."

The tobacco industry also maintains that it has never manipulated the level of nicotine in cigarettes. But the Food and Drug Administration (FDA) asserts that the reason so many cigarette smokers find it almost impossible to quit is because the industry deliberately adds nicotine — a potent addicting agent — during the cigarette production process. Most Americans would be surprised to learn that companies spray on nicotine in addition to the nicotine already found in tobacco. Over 77 percent of all smokers, according to the FDA, want to quit but cannot because of the overpowering effects of nicotine.

According to the National Institute on Drug Abuse, nicotine is as addictive as heroin and five to ten times more potent than cocaine or morphine in altering mood behavior. The tobacco lobby has, of course, claimed for years that it does not manipulate nicotine levels. Internal industry documents, disclosed in lawsuits with the industry, contradict these statements. These documents show that R.J. Reynolds company, the nation's largest cigarette maker, altered the level of nicotine in order to increase the "kick" of its Winston brand and make it more competitive with Phillip Morris which had a high level of nicotine in its Marlboro brand.

In 1995, the *Wall Street Journal* disclosed a 1991 document from the Brown & Williamson company that said cigarette companies added ammonia to its cigarettes. The effect of this, according to the document, is "associated with increases in impact and satisfaction reported by smokers." Ammonia enhances the level of nicotine delivered to the bloodstream and makes the smoking experience more addictive; it increases the punch of the cigarette.

The fact that Phillip Morris added ammonia to its popular Marlboro and Kool brands was cause for concern for RJ Reynolds company. In a 1973 memo, a company researcher observed: "Marlboro and Kool smokes contain more ... nicotine than our comparable blends, hence would be expected to show more 'kick' than our brands." The memo recommended that RJ Reynolds develop a cigarette using ammonia to enhance nicotine. "Because brands of the new type continue to show vigorous growth in sales; because a high proportion of beginning smokers are learning to like Marlboro, the leading brand of the new type; and because we have no current brand in this newly identified, major segment of the market; it has become appropriate for us to consider moving our present brands in the direction of the new type of cigarette."

New York Times columnist Bob Herbert recounts the story of a model who posed for cigarette ads. The model asked R.J. Reynolds executives if any of them smoke. The reply: "Are you kidding? We reserve that right for the poor, the young, the black and the stupid."

The disingenuous and cavalier behavior of Big Tobacco obscures the fact that smoking is the greatest public health threat the country faces. Each day in America 3,000 children begin to smoke and eventually 1,000 of them will die as a result. Tobacco is the leading cause of death in the nation, with over 400,000 deaths every year. Although the incidence of smoking for the population as a whole has decreased in the last twenty years, teen smoking is on the rise. The average age to begin smoking is eleven to twelve, so prevention is particularly important for children at younger ages.

Recognizing the enormity of the public health threat, some states and localities have taken aggressive action to curb the power of the tobacco industry. The Attorney Generals in states like Minnesota and Massachusetts have pursued aggressive litigation designed to recapture the health costs incurred because of smoking deaths and debilitations. The Attorney General in New Jersey has not been visible or aggressive in this litigation.

Many states have strongly challenged the tobacco industry's ability to market to teenagers. California enacted a massive anti-smoking advertising campaign aimed at stopping teen smoking and the state has recently banned tobacco advertisements near schools. Many localities have innovative programs. Woodridge, Illinois and Newton, Massachusetts, have begun to license cigarette retailers — implementing tough penalties and enforcing them with spot checks by undercover buyers.

Before the campaign, 87 percent of stores sold to minors; after the measures were implemented, no sales to minors were found. In Santa Rosa California, merchants are required to keep cigarettes behind counters. In Brookline, Massachusetts cigarette vending machines are banned. In Preston, Minnesota, ads in cigarette stores are banned.

New Jersey lags behind all these states in innovative anti-tobacco measures. In Princeton I was unable to persuade local government to conduct sting operations to stop selling to minors. Big Tobacco loves New Jersey.

The love affair begins with massive contributions to both political parties. The tobacco companies are routinely among the biggest contributors to both Democrats and Republicans. In 1995, for example, Phillip Morris donated $105,000 to the Republican leadership and $92,500 to the Democratic leadership. This does not include additional hundreds of thousands of dollars to individual candidates and soft money to the parties. The tobacco lobby is so brazen in New Jersey that its chief lobbyist, Dale Florio, is also the campaign chair of a Republican congressman and one of the key advisors to Republicans statewide.

Tobacco is so influential in New Jersey that the state still invests pension money in tobacco corporations. In 1997, the last year data are available, New Jersey invested almost $241 million of public pension money in Philip Morris Companies. Other government entities have divested all tobacco holdings and New Jersey should too.

New Jersey's lackluster efforts to control tobacco became evident in a recent federal study of the ability of teenagers to buy cigarettes in all fifty states. In the typical state, four out of 10 teenagers successfully left convenience stores, gas stations, and groceries with what officials call the No. 1 threat to their health. Half the states did better than that and half did worse. In New Jersey 44.4 percent of the teens who attempted to buy tobacco were successful. Aggressive enforcement in several states — including Florida, New Hampshire and Maine — has reduced the incidence of teens buying cigarettes to less than 20 percent. Don't New Jersey teenagers deserve equal protection?

We need to get tobacco money out of New Jersey politics and we need to stop investing public money in Big Tobacco. Ultimately, Congress should not sign any tobacco settlement unless it contains serious penalties for failing to bring down the rate of teen smoking. Congress should also refuse to surrender the power of the FDA to regulate nicotine as a drug and Congress should not limit the liability of tobacco companies for their actions. Until tough new measures are conceived and implemented, each day in New Jersey 100 teenagers will start to smoke and seventy percent will never stop.

CHAPTER THIRTEEN

GARDEN STATE SHAKEDOWN

"A great democracy must be progressive or it will soon cease to be great or a democracy"
— Theodore Roosevelt, The New Nationalism.

"The future is not for party's 'playing politics,' but for measures conceived in the largest spirit, pushed by parties whose leaders are statesman, not demagogues, who love not their offices, but their duty and their opportunity for service."
— Woodrow Wilson

The political heritage of New Jersey is one of the most wild and colorful in the nation. The Garden State has, alternatively, been a bastion of democratic reform and a corruption pit. Currently, New Jersey politics is in one of its most depraved modes, badly in need of reclaiming its substantial progressive heritage.

The most ignominious Governor in New Jersey history was the British Lord Cornbury who served as Governor in the Colonial period from 1703 to 1708. According to a nineteenth century history, complaints of the people compelled the Queen to revoke his commission. A contemporary described his rule: "[H]is behavior was trifling, mean and extravagant. It was not uncommon for him to dress himself in a woman's habit, and then to patrol the fort in which he resided. Such freaks of low humor exposed him to the universal contempt of the people; but their indignation was kindled by his despotic rule, savage bigotry, insatiable avarice, and injustice, not only to the public, but even to his private creditors."

This despotism was, of course, succeeded by many of the most important battles of the American Revolution and for a time the Continental Congress met in New Jersey, which almost became the capitol of the nation. Central New Jersey was in many ways crucible for the revolutionary and democratic ideals of the eighteenth century.

Graft in the Garden State began with Alexander Hamilton — the most anti-democratic Founding Father — who recognized New Jersey as strategically located between New York City and Philadelphia, and a state in which business interests could rule. The railroads were the first key interest group in the nineteenth century. The first railroad, the Camden & Amboy, obtained a monopoly on rail service and a generous tax exemption form the legislature; this enterprise, and its successor the Pennsylvania Railroad, routinely bribed governors, congressman, and senators. If rival railroads wanted to do business in the Garden State, they had to buy their own politicians. The Republican Party came to represent the Pennsylvania Railroad and the Democrats represented the liquor lobby, the racetrack syndicates, and the Baltimore and Ohio Railroad.

At the end of the nineteenth century, New Jersey coddled corporations. A young lawyer, James B. Dill, backed by key political and business figures, established the Corporation Trust Company of New Jersey. For a fee, the company helped businesses incorporate in New Jersey and permitted giant holding companies at a time when other states were outlawing these holding companies for their anti-monopolistic practices. (Rockefeller's Standard Oil was an example of an outlawed trust.) By incorporating in New Jersey, the giant trusts of the day could avoid regulation and taxes imposed by other states.

New Jersey was considered such a center of corruption and influence peddling that it was featured in a famous 1905 McLure's magazine series by noted muckraker Lincoln Steffens. (Steffens became famous for his expose of urban corruption: *The Shame of the Cities*.) In *New Jersey: A Traitor State*, Steffens charged that "New Jersey is selling out the rest of us. " He wrote about the "stench of the vice graft," and he imagined New Jersey speaking to corporations: "The other states have made your business a crime; we'll license you to break their laws. We'll sell out the whole United States to you, and cheap, and our courts are 'safe' and our legislature is 'liberal' and our location is convenient."

Steffens' muckraking helped encourage a reform wing of the New Jersey Republican party called the "New Idea." Although the reform wing was defeated at the polls in the beginning of the century, when Woodrow Wilson was elected Governor in 1910 he rode on the coattails of a burgeoning progressive movement and vowed to curb corporate power. He delivered on his promise by passing seven bills — known as the Seven Sisters — that got New Jersey out of the incorporation business, and put tight controls on New Jersey companies. Violations were punished by charter revocation or criminal prosecution of directors. Wilson also rammed through an amazing battery of progressive legislation that promoted direct democracy, undermined the power of the country bosses, and reformed New Jersey's campaign finance system.

It has been all downhill since Wilson. The county bosses and corporate interests today control New Jersey to such a degree that, by any yardstick, New Jersey has one of the least robust democracies in the country. New Jersey has no initiative and referendum, so citizens here do not have the opportunity to decide their own future, as citizens in many other states do. Campaign fundraising rules are notoriously lax in New Jersey, and almost no controls are placed on gift giving and lobbyists. A national survey of lobbying activity in the 50 states found that New Jersey, along with roughly 15 other states, has the least restrictive lobbying laws in the country. While most states limit the ability of lobbyists to make campaign contributions, restrict the ability of elected officials to approach lobbyists for donations and restrict giving from lobbyists to elected officials, New Jersey has no such limits. The penalties for failure to register or violate state law are merely small fines, compared to tough criminal sanctions in other states, and there is no registration required of local government lobbying. The special interests just keep rolling along in New Jersey, spending $16 million on lobbying each year.

New Jersey possesses very few restrictions on campaign cash and its election laws are uniquely designed to forestall reform and democratic participation. New Jersey law allows elected officials to hold unlimited multiple offices; it allows direct corporate contributions; it permits unlimited gifts from corporate or any other donor to politicians; it has a moribund election law enforcement agency whose budget is repeatedly cut; and it permits the tax deductibility of lobbying expenses. Lobbyists outnumber legislators in New Jersey by a ratio of 4.79 to one (575 to 120).

The federal government has frequently investigated New Jersey's campaign financing system: a former top advisor to New Jersey's Governor was indicted for improperly linking municipal bond offerings to political favors, which led to a federal investigation of cash-for-favors in the municipal bond industry in New Jersey. A corporation linked to a former Governor's chief of staff was indicted and convicted on criminal charges of awarding cash for government lottery contracts. The current Governor has been criticized for tolerating questionable soft money practices.

The key to New Jersey politics is the unholy alliance between the corporate special interests and the county bosses. Everything is controlled at the county level. In a 1998 series called "Pay to Play," the *Home News and Tribune* explained how the system works in one county that happens to be controlled by Democrats. "The well-oiled money machine known as the Middlesex County Democratic Party takes in large donations from many of the major professional organization hired by the county and its municipalities. The money is used to secure the Democrats power base in the county... Contributors are paid back handsomely with lucrative contracts and the smug knowledge that they have a virtual stranglehold on professional services in their fields in Middlesex County." The newspaper concluded that "Democrats Buy It All in Middlesex County."

The paper goes on to explain: "The losers in this insiders' club are the citizens, who taxes pay for inflated professional contracts and whose towns or county rarely hire anyone outside the network, even if those outsiders might be innovative or cheaper. The Democrats own Middlesex County. Current state laws make that monopoly even stronger. The law perpetuates the old buddy network of lawyers, developers, engineers and other professional who see the county as a cash cow."

For example, in Middlesex county between 1993 and 1997, contractors — who do business with the county and municipalities — contributed $1.75 million to the Democratic party, about 43 percent of everything Democrats raised. In other counties, where Republicans are in control (like Somerset, where Governor Whitman is from), the same "pay to play" system is in place. Statewide fund-raising by the county parties jumped from $5 million in 1992 to $9.4 million in 1996.

The grip that the bosses have on the twenty-one counties in New Jersey extends even to the selection of candidates for office. In truth, there is no democracy in New Jersey. Candidates for virtually every office are handpicked by the county bosses and power brokers in each county. Rather than have open primaries, like virtually every other state in the nation, the New Jersey system allows the county chair to handpick the Democratic or Republican candidate for any office. (Some county organizations pick the candidate through conventions that are rigged or have few rules.) Hardly anyone ever challenges the county organization's choice for a party nomination.

This leads to the bizarre spectacle of voters going into a primary booth and having the "choice" of only one candidate. In the latest primary elections in Mercer county, for example, the taxpayers shelled out thousands to go to the polls and find only one candidate to choose from for multiple offices: Congress, Freeholder, Town Council, etc. In other words, most of the time the primary voters from each party can vote for whomever they like, as long as it is the person selected by the county bosses. Just like under the old Soviet system, you can have any ice cream flavor you want as long as it is vanilla.

Perhaps the most accomplished practitioner of County hardball politics is John Lynch, the *de facto* boss of Middlesex County and the former leader of the Democratic Senate majority. Lynch is a diminutive, wiry man in his late fifties who constantly has a cell phone to his ear. If you want anything done in Central New Jersey, he is the man to see. Lynch is probably the smartest operative in New Jersey politics and has perfected the art of wrangling contributions from corporate special interests. He is a man of his word, most of the time. (As smart as he is, Lynch has missed the fundamental point that the Democrats will never be able to match the Republicans in fundraising, so the party might as well try something new like standing for campaign finance reform rather than trying to compete economically. Lynch and the Democrats have never learned that lesson and keep spending millions to be the minority party year after year.)

The refreshing thing about Lynch is his occasional candor about how the Garden State Shakedown works. When Lynch was Senate president he confessed that in 1991 he posted a bill for a vote in response to campaign contributions lavished on Senators by optometrists. (The bill authorized optometrists to dispense certain types of eye medication.) After Lynch made this admission, the Republicans filed an ethics complaint against him. This caused Lynch to threaten to tell-all about how money buys votes in New Jersey. The Republicans, in turn, were so shocked that a politician might speak the truth about government in New Jersey that they backed down from

167

the ethics investigation. One Republican admitted to a reporter: "It [filing ethics charges against Lynch] was an incredibly stupid thing to do."

In a speech, Lynch said of the ethics investigation:

"At last, we will have a forum where leaders, under oath and subject to cross-examination, will talk about what we politicians like to call 'access,' when reality says money creates influence."

"We'll talk about such major public policy initiatives as tort reform, where a leading advocate was the tobacco industry and where massive political contributions have been made by the tobacco industry to leaders advancing the tort reform legislation."

"We'll talk about co-generation legislation and how advocates for it made very significant political contributions and, perhaps coincidentally, co-generation legislation was approved in 1992."

"We'll talk about the whole world of health-care legislation and the thousands upon thousands of dollars pumped into political parties by those who benefitted from health care legislation."

"We'll talk about many specifics involving legislation that was posted and voted upon where, perhaps coincidentally, significant campaign contributions were made by those advocating that legislation. Perhaps it's not a coincidence at all."

The Democratic party in the state, which used to

be the reform party under Woodrow Wilson, has abandoned any reform impulse. In an article entitled "New Jersey Democrats See 'Soft Money' As A Necessary Evil," the *New York Times* related how Alan Karcher, former gubernatorial candidate and chair of Mercer County Democrats, confided: "[I]t is a system designed to chill the ordinary citizens participation in terms of being a candidate and in fund-raising. The whole fund-raising atmosphere has gotten so out of hand, but if you don't do it, you know your opponents are out there doing it. It's an unpleasant battle for survival."

There are essentially no rules in campaign financing in New Jersey. In 1994 the State Democratic Party, for example, was concerned that all of its assets would be seized by the Postal Service as part of a lawsuit charging the state Democrats with abuse of postal permits in 1989.

Fearful of seizure, the Democrats simply had big contributors funnel money to county organizations (which have no limits on spending). Big donors like the Walt Disney company poured "soft" dollars into the Mercer County Democratic party, which in turn could finance help for federal races. Not only did this avoid the $1,000 per person limit in federal races, but the state party did not have to worry that any of its assets would be seized.

So, for example, in 1994, according to a review of state party records, nine corporations funneled over $129,000 into the Mercer County organization which then used most of this money to fund the statewide efforts of New Jersey's Senate and 13 congressional races.

The Republicans do exactly the same thing, and they have had their share of embarrassing revelations. In 1997 it emerged that a New Jersey businessman, who once testified he worked for the Korean CIA and whose donations have been returned by top-ranking Republicans, gave over $17,000 to New Jersey Republicans between 1994 and 1997.

Even when there is some "reform" of the system, it turns out to be sham reform. In New Jersey, so-called campaign finance reforms are nothing but window-dressing. A supposed reform in 1993, for example, did nothing but require reporting of gifts, not their ban, and actually made it easier for companies to give money to the leaders of both political parties. The same bill cut the budget of the agency charged with enforcing violations of the campaign finance laws.

The great New Jersey Gravy Train rolls on and on. The lobbyists keep the casinos humming. And the Garden State Shakedown keeps getting bigger and bigger. For the citizens who don't have a seat on the Gravy Train, the Shakedown keeps getting more and more expensive. How expensive will it have to get before the voters demand the fundamental reforms that citizens in other states already enjoy? Only then will New Jersey live up to the ideal expressed in Article One of its Constitution that "all political power is inherent in the people."

CHAPTER FOURTEEN

ALL POWER IS INHERENT
IN THE PEOPLE

"All political power is inherent in the people. Government is instituted for the protection, security and benefit of the people, and they have the right at all times to alter or reform the same, whenever the public good may require it."
— NJ Constitution, Article 1, Section 2(a)

"He who does not increase his knowledge, decreases it; he who does not seek to acquire wisdom, forfeits his life."
— Hillel

The road to political reform in New Jersey, and in the nation, is a long, arduous path. Two measures are essential. The first is to ensure that citizens have more complete information about, and easier access to, government. The second requires fundamental campaign finance reform. Without these basic changes, the Garden State Shakedown continue. Any reforms must also be enacted at the local, state and national level because all three levels of politics inevitably intersect.

Mega-corporations are executing plans to transmit hundreds of channels of entertainment — and countless commercial products — into every American home. There are no plans, however, to upgrade a democratic infrastructure that has never been more decrepit. Any voter knows that most polling machines date back decades, reflecting the low priority placed on citizen participation. The voting registration requirements of virtually every state are not only arcane but, when combined with ancient mechanisms for recording and storing voting records, discourage participation and citizen involvement.

Modern technology allows us to shop, to obtain credit, and to perform highly personal and important tasks over the phone lines. When are America's political parties going to allow voter registration over the phone or via computer or television? It can hardly be said that today's archaic paper ballots prevent chicanery, as witnessed by several invalidated fraudulent elections in the last election cycles (particularly in New Jersey and Pennsylvania).

New technologies could also more readily provide information to the citizenry. Slowly, the federal government is placing records on-line for citizen access. But many members of Congress don't even have web sites. Government at all levels needs to be brought up to date.

The information superhighway could allow citizens more easily to communicate their ideas to elected representatives rather than the other way around. Consider how Congress does business. Each member is allocated at least a half million of our tax dollars to communicate with constituents. This money is now exclusively spent sending out self-aggrandizing literature that serves as re-election flyers. Requiring that the money be spent to promote communication the other way might help re-acquaint Capitol Hill with Main Street. Congressional franking privileges should be scrapped and instead Congress should create 800 numbers and web sites that will allow citizens from anywhere, including public libraries, instantly to communicate their ideas and to receive a record of the voting performance of their elected representative.

Evolving technologies can not only allow citizens to receive and send information to elected representatives, but to communicate with one another. The New England Town meeting was the model of democratic governance adopted by our forefathers; this idea can be partly resuscitated by the latest technologies.

Nobody denies that our democratic system needs

refurbishing. America has the lowest voter turnout of any industrialized nation. The polls show that Americans are more distrustful of political institutions than at any time in the nation's history. Government has produced a Markets 2000 report that analyzes how to update the stock markets for the turn of the century. We need a Democracy 2000 report to update how to bring our democracy up to speed in the next century. What is required is a blue-level commission — perhaps comprised of past Presidents — committed to making this country as technologically advanced in its democracy as it is in its industry. (Making democracy more deliberative, as envisioned by the Framers of the Constitution, is even more important in an era when television distorts the debate.)

The key to reclaiming our democracy is fundamental campaign finance reform. In every state where there has been a popular initiative to limit the amount of money in politics, the initiative passed by an overwhelming majority. In Maine, voters adopted a "Clean Money" election scheme that provides for public financing of state elections for those candidates who agree to forgo private donations. The Connecticut legislature voted to ban all soft-money. And the Vermont legislature enacted a public financing scheme as well.

Ultimately, the only solution to the massive influence-peddling in American politics is a national scheme of public financing supported by a voluntary taxpayer check-off mechanism. Americans would willingly pay to secure clean and honest elections. A few dollars per person would be a small price to pay to restore our democracy and to make our electoral system a model for nations throughout the world.

Several other changes to the system of financing campaigns would radically reduce the influence of corporate interests:

1. Provide reasonable amounts of free radio and TV time for candidates who qualify for the ballot by collecting the requisite number of signatures. America is the only advanced industrial nation that does not provide free media time to candidates. Media costs are the predominant expense in campaigns.

2. Shorten the election cycle to eight weeks. Other industrialized nations have condensed campaign periods: seventeen days in the United Kingdom and three to five weeks in Denmark, for example. By shortening the length of the cycle, the perpetual hunt for campaign money would be reduced.

3. Amend the constitution to permit limiting the amount of money spent on campaigns. Such an amendment would establish the principle that money is not constitutionally protected speech. Unless an amendment is enacted, limits on spending cannot be legislated under the Supreme Court's decision in *Buckley v. Valeo*. This is a necessary precondition to establishing absolute spending and contribution limits to political campaigns. The United States is one of only three western democracies that neither features public financing of elections nor limits the amount a federal candidate may spend.

4. Enact term limits. This reduces the concentration of

power in the hands of a few and presents fewer opportunities for special interests to influence powerful, entrenched legislators. We should limit congressional terms to six (twelve years) and senatorial terms to two (twelve years). Term limits have enjoyed bipartisan support over the years: Abraham Lincoln, Harry Truman, Dwight Eisenhower and John Kennedy all supported the idea.

5. End the franked mail system of incumbent protection for Congressmen and implement the Canadian system which allows all citizens to mail, for free, a letter to their representative. Franked mail is predominantly self-aggrandizing re-election material and Members of Congress are now permitted to mail out $500,000 per year at taxpayer expense. Reversing this system by adopting the Canadian approach would re-establish the principle that Congress is the servant, not the master, of the citizenry.

6. Amend the Constitution to limit the First Amendment rights of corporations to engage in political speech. The amendment would make it clear that corporations are not "persons" for constitutional purposes and therefore do not have the same constitutional protections as individuals. Once this Amendment was passed, the federal government would have greater power to regulate the political activities of corporations and impose restrictions on their political contributions.

7. Declare election day a national holiday. This would enhance voter turnout and therefore dilute the effects of money in politics. Most advanced western nations con-

duct their elections on weekends or declare election day a holiday. America's failure to do so partially explains why we have the lowest turnout rate of any western industrial democracy.

8. Change cumbersome and Byzantine voter registration laws to increase participation and further dilute the role of money. Same day registration should be approved immediately and the government should set a goal of universal registration.

9. Ban "soft-money" contributions to political parties. This so-called "soft money" allows special interests to circumvent the current meager restrictions on campaign. There are no limits set on direct individual or corporate contributions to political parties.

10. Expand the powers of the Federal Election Commission. The Commission should be given criminal prosecution powers.

11. End lobbying by foreign corporations and agents. Make it illegal for foreign corporations or entities to attempt to influence American legislation either directly or indirectly. We must also shut the revolving door and forbid former elected representatives from taking money from foreign interests.

In many ways, there is no such thing as politics in America anymore. Much of what we characterize as politics has become a near full-time fundraising business. (To many political leaders, this is not a problem. Consider Newt Gingrich's position: "One of the greatest myths in modern politics is that campaigns are too expensive. The political process is in fact, not overfunded, but under-funded.")

We can no longer afford to have the lowest rate of political participation of any western industrial democracy. In Sweden, for example, the woman next in line to be Prime Minister resigned because she had charged several parking tickets and some diapers to a government credit card. Imagine if those standards of probity existed on Capitol Hill?

The administration of Woodrow Wilson and the surging progressive movement in New Jersey at the beginning of the century set the benchmark for progressive movements around the country. Efforts to end the abuse of child labor, reform the campaign finance laws, and break the power of monopolies all created important legacies for the state of New Jersey. At the close of the twentieth century, it is time to rediscover those legacies in a deeper sense. Even today, the state has some of the most liberal laws and legal opinions protecting the rights of citizens and minorities, but a closed political system uniquely susceptible to special interest pressure. The challenge is to resurrect New Jersey's history of reform and use it to improve our lives.

In order to do this, however, we must get more people involved in politics at all levels. People have dropped out of democracy because they don't believe they can make a difference. We must make them believe.

It is more important than ever for citizens to get involved in our democracy because the challenges are so

great. The end of the twentieth century is similar to the
end of the nineteenth century, except today, rather than
jump from state to state to avoid regulation and laws,
many companies jump from country to country. We need
creative ways to combat the rise of unregulated global
corporations with its attendant consequences on people's
lives.

The Framers of the Constitution established a division between the three branches of government: executive, legislative and judicial. But they never foresaw the
power of insurance companies, HMO's, tobacco companies, real estate interests and other powerful private
actors to hijack our government and become almost a
fourth branch of government. The twentieth century has
largely been about working out solutions to the problem
of private economic power that the Framers never envisioned. New Jersey has a great tradition of giving citizens
the tools to control their own destiny, influenced by Louis
Brandies and other progressives who realized the importance of using the law to achieve democratic reforms.
Other states have reformed their campaign finance laws,
as have other countries, as has New Jersey in its history.
The only obstacle to reform today is a lack of political
will.

Roughly 100 years ago Woodrow Wilson delivered
his formative speech calling upon citizens to act "In the
Nation's service." Wilson's ideas, as expressed in his book
The New Freedom, are no less valid at the end of the century than they were at the beginning: "There has now
come over the land," Wilson said, "that un-American set
of conditions which enables a small number of men who
control the government to get favors from the govern-

ment."

Wilson's solution was equally valid: "Nations are renewed from the bottom, not from the top; that the genius which springs up from the ranks of the unknown men is the genius which renews the youth and energy of the people."

POSTSCRIPT

GENERATION L — LEADERS

"Be not like servants who serve their master for the sake of receiving a reward; be rather like servants who serve their master without thought of a reward."
— Antigonos of Socho, disciple of Simon the Just

"Aggressive Fighting for the Right is the Noblest sport the world affords."
— Theodore Roosevelt

Adlai Stevenson was campaigning in Chicago, when a woman approached him and said: "Mr. Stevenson, I so much enjoyed your talk this evening, really I did; I found your comments absolutely superfluous." Stevenson smiled, thanked her, and tried to move on as rapidly as possible. But the woman, not to be denied, grabbed him by the elbow and said, "Really, I mean it Mr. Stevenson, your talk was so important, you must have it published and widely distributed." Stevenson replied: "Well, we have made arrangements to have my remarks published posthumously," and the lady responded, "Excellent. The sooner, the better."

Received wisdom is that politics in America is superfluous and one should talk about it in a posthumous sense. I don't believe this. Politics in America is critical to the future of our county.

One of my favorite professors at Princeton University taught me in a course on Ancient and Medieval political theory that politics comes from the Greek word "polis," which means community. Many today have a vested interest in fostering cynicism about politics, particularly the corporate lobbyists who control the government. To me, politics is about making the community better.

This book is based on my twenty years of experience in politics in New Jersey, the last six of which have been in electoral politics. I wrote this book for the citizens of New Jersey. I want to thank each of them for listening to my ideas over the years and sharing their own. The highest honor I ever received was to be elected to the Princeton Township Committee. Public service is a public trust and the highest reward is to serve the people. Serving the people is compensation in itself. I believe in democracy and the citizenry, and particularly in the willingness of young people to take an active role in shaping society.

My ancestors were immigrants to this country. They had to leave behind their homes and possessions in Europe and they never enjoyed the liberties that we do in this nation. When I reflect upon their experiences I always give thanks not just for the liberties that we all enjoy, but for the opportunity to represent the people. We all have an obligation to improve the society in which we live; the obligation is even stronger for those called upon to serve.

I was very fortunate to grow up in a family in which the discussion of social and political issues was considered crucial. The talk at the dinner table was less about what happened to you than about what you thought could be done to improve society. One of my grandfathers had worked with Eleanor Roosevelt, campaigned for Adlai Stevenson, and had been active with Robert and John Kennedy. My other grandfather always participated in progressive political causes. My mother frequently volunteered at hospitals and other good institutions, and my father was involved in many progressive political causes.

Probably my independent political nature traces its roots to my ancestors who came from Luxembourg, an obscure European nation known principally for being stubborn enough never to join the federation of German states. The motto of the country: "We stand as we are." My determined nature manifested itself early. Prior to enrolling at Princeton University, my best friend and I set out to bicycle cross-country. We had planned a trip from Portland, Oregon to New York City. When our bicycles were put on the wrong bus, we arrived unprepared, with no maps and few spare parts, in Seattle, Washington. Undeterred, we made the journey to New York City in thirty-two days, averaging 100 miles per day.

I received my first opportunity in politics in 1978 when Ralph Nader offered me a summer job in Washington D.C. I helped to start a publication called the *Multinational Monitor* which tracks the activities of corporations around the globe. Working with Nader was the best job I ever had in politics. I was fortunate enough to meet many public interest activists who work long hours devoted to the public good. It was while working for Nader that I developed a passion for creative ideas and fighting for the underdog to add to my already stubborn heritage.

The lessons I learned from that era always stuck with me. At the time I co-authored a book published by the Sierra Club Press entitled *Public Domain, Private Dominion.* The book called for an end to giveaways that cost taxpayers over $10 billion every year. I remember testifying before Congress to overturn an ancient law that, to this day, is on the books and allows mining companies — even foreign ones — to take gold and silver from our public lands for free. I was virtually the only person in the hearing room (other than the elected officials) who was not a lobbyist. The congressmen demonstrated a bipartisan indifference to my pleas for reform, discussing their golf game throughout most of my testimony. I vowed to do more in the future to make the system more accountable to the people.

After stints at Chicago Law School and Harvard Law School I clerked for a Federal District Court judge. I was subsequently offered a position as a law professor at Hofstra University; truly an outstanding opportunity. The ability to influence future generations is a real honor and I came to appreciate teaching as a noble profession.

While I was teaching law, I got involved in legal cases that could have a public interest impact. I helped environmental groups bring a shareholder action that required Exxon corporation to build double-hulled tankers so that an incident like the Valdez oil spill did not occur again. I helped in another action that successfully persuaded the Dupont corporation to eliminate all CFC production by the year 1996 so as to stop harming the ozone layer and contributing to global warming.

In 1991 I tried a small case on my own behalf challenging the tobacco companies. After an airline refused to honor my non-smoking ticket and placed me in a smoking section I requested a simple apology. Failing to receive one, I brought a legal action with the intention of creating a precedent. *Carl J. Mayer v. Air France* created a precedent that will permit passengers to bring tort and contract actions against airlines for secondhand smoke injury. Secondhand smoke is recognized by the EPA as an environmental hazard that kills or injures 53,000 people per year and is one of the leading preventable causes of death in the United States.

While teaching and litigating, however, I began to understand the importance of getting involved in electoral politics in order to truly make a difference. I was elected to the Princeton Township Committee in 1994, the first Independent elected in the history of Princeton. I was honored to receive the endorsement at the time of the New Jersey Environmental Federation, the Sierra Club, the National Organization for Women and my local County Women's Political Caucus.

As a local elected official I tried to remain true to my roots of fighting for the underdog with creative ideas and an independent determination to do what is right. I have always told it like it is in politics. I would rather lose an election than mislead the voters or bow to the power of special interests.

Apart from coming to understand the power of corporate lobbyists, I also learned that few of the conventional ideas about how Americans view politics are true. Conventional thinking is that government employees and bureaucrats are lazy and uninvolved. The reality is that some of the most dedicated workers in America work for the government, often at the local level. Conventional wisdom is that Americans do not care about politics; in reality, they care deeply.

The stereotype is that government employees are unproductive and unhelpful. My experience as an elected official suggests the opposite. Consider Pat S., the clerk of Princeton Township. The town would not run without her. In addition to her myriad daily duties, she spends many late nights, often until 2 a.m., taking the minutes and ensuring that local government meetings run smoothly. Pat had a mild heart attack during my tenure on the Township committee. She is so dedicated to Princeton that almost as soon as she awoke in her hospital bed, she wanted her Princeton Township work to be given to her. She wanted to go back immediately to work in Town Hall; only after doctors insisted did she relent. But within days she was back on the job, as dedicated as ever.

Consider also, Bob C. Bob works in the public works department in Princeton. He is a deaf mute. Most employees of Princeton get to work between 8:30 a.m. and 9 a.m. Bob gets in at 7 a.m. If he does not have work to do at that time, he begins to do the work of his fellow employees. Bob hasn't missed a day of work for Princeton Township in thirteen years. Other employees have stayed home because ice or snow prevented them from driving to work. Not Bob. He bicycles to work because he doesn't have a drivers license. Bob has bicycled to work in the rain, the snow, the sleet and every other type of weather.

Bob has been frustrated working for local government, because he could only work five days a week. When Princeton Township decided to commence a seven-day-a-week recycling program, Bob volunteered to do the program on weekends. Now he works seven days a week for the community. There may be few people in America who are as dedicated to their community and job as Bob C., but in my experience most employees of local government are devoted, helpful, and efficient.

Over the years as an activist and elected official, I have seen countless individuals give of their time, energy, money, and intellect to advance important causes in their neighborhoods here in New Jersey. Their only reward is improving our common social condition.

Consider Mary P., a mother, career woman, and activist on a mission. She is a one-woman dynamo. Mary and her husband live two towns away from my hometown of Princeton. Nobody can determine how she finds the time for her busy private and work life, so people were amazed when she volunteered to lead the charge against the Ogden-Martin corporation after the company announced plans to build an incinerator in Mercer county.

Nothing deterred Mary P. She, along with citizens from towns all over Central New Jersey, got together and organized night after night. I saw Mary at literally hundreds of hearings, meetings, and political events. Mary was tireless. One night the incinerator company and the Wall Street Banks that backed them paid hundreds of supporters to come to a county Freeholder meeting where elected officials were holding yet another hearing on the incinerator. So many people were crammed in the room that proponents of the incinerator were able to block the door. To gain entrance to the hearing room, one had to answer the question of whether they were for or against the incinerator. People opposed to the incinerator were told they were not welcome. This did not deter Mary. She made it into the room despite the intimidation and made an impassioned plea against the project.

After many years and enormous patience the project was exposed as a White Elephant and elected leaders had no choice but to vote it down. Were it not for Mary and her fellow citizens, the economic and environmental landscape of Central New Jersey would be dramatically different.

Despite what political pundits say about citizens being disengaged from politics and public life, I have witnessed countless Americans deeply involved in their communities and in public issues. I am particularly heartened by the many young people who put themselves on the line to make society better: The Rutgers student who tirelessly canvasses door to door opposing nuclear power plants; the women outside a voting booth who said she would say a prayer while voting so that I and other elected officials would make the right decisions.

A real inspiration was a young man in his mid-twenties who worked racking shopping carts for a supermarket; while I was campaigning one night he approached me and said he used to work for an oil refinery in northern New Jersey. He said that every few weeks the bottom of the oil tanks would have to be changed because the oil created holes in the tanks. He wanted to know what damage the oil was causing to the ground underneath the tanks. "You should look into that," he said. "I'm willing to help."

There are many who are willing to help. We have to give them back their democracy.

AFTERWORD

THE DEATH OF THE CORPORATION

"If we are ever to get corporations to act as 'a responsible individual' ... we will need to attach full responsibility to the human beings who speak and act for it..."

— Admiral Hyman Rickover,
Defense Expenditure Hearings, 1982

An irony of contemporary politics is that as corporate special interests enjoy the greatest power they have ever had over the political process, the future leaders of society have never been more disenchanted with traditional corporate institutions. The challenge is not only to end the dominance of corporate interests over the political system, but to remake the political system to respond to the needs of individuals and new institutions.

The texture of society has changed greatly. Not only have urban problems migrated to the suburbs, but the sense of community in late twentieth century New Jersey is very different from what it was at the beginning of the century. This is primarily because the nature of the central institution of society, the corporation, has changed. Americans are losing confidence in what has been the central institution of our society for much of the nation's history: the corporation.

Although numerous Americans work for a company, many believe that these organizations are not delivering and make unrealistic demands on employees and their families. Massive layoffs by leading Fortune 500 companies are only the latest reminder of the fragility of corporate existence. If working for a company means job insecurity, an uncertain pension, tenuous health insurance, lost privacy and brutal commutes, Americans will continue to drop out of the corporate structure. Thirty-six percent of the labor force does some work at home, and that figure is expected to reach fifty percent by the year 2000. In many respects, corporations have become dinosaurs in the age of mammals.

Throughout American history, the corporation has been society's most important institution. Corporate entities discovered the nation. The Company of Massachusetts Bay in New England, for example, was a vehicle for John Winthrop and the Puritans to achieve religious freedom, to secure distance from the British Crown, and to conduct an experiment in self-governance. In the earliest years of the Republic corporations were imbued with a public purpose and built the nascent infrastructure projects of the day: turnpikes, canals, and roadways. By the end of the nineteenth century, many Americans believed, corporations had lost their public purpose and become ungovernable private behemoths. (John D. Rockefeller's Standard Oil monopoly and J.P. Morgan's railroad oligopolies symbolized the problem.)

Although measures were taken to tame corporate excesses, including anti-trust, environmental, and labor laws, the corporation became even more prominent in the twentieth century. For much of this century, the corporation was the lynchpin of social contract: in return for allegiance to the company, citizens could expect lifetime employment, full benefits, and a pension. (General Motors chairman Alfred Sloan succinctly characterized the bargain with his celebrated formula: "What is good for General Motors is good for America"). The large American corporation became a surrogate family, a surrogate community, and a surrogate culture.

Most of the other institutions in society imitated the corporation: charitable, educational , sports, and religious organizations adopted corporate morays, including the Board of Directors structure. The corporation — particularly large Fortune 500 multinationals — set the tone and created the values for a nation that never had the strong cultural, religious, and state traditions of older societies.

As the century ends, however, the corporate social compact is null and void. What is good for General Motors is good for General Motors, not necessarily for the United States. Fortune 500 corporations have not provided one net new job in this country for twenty years, and when one prominent business magazine recently printed an article on how to get ahead in the new business world, it quoted a middle-manager: "This is the nineties: you have to screw the corporation before the corporation screws you."

Corporations no longer have the allegiance of society's leaders. Fortune 500 executives are leaving management positions to begin their own enterprises; the best and brightest business school students are rejecting corporate life for other opportunities. In a survey conducted by a leading bank, over forty percent of America's wealthiest executives revealed that they would not choose the corporate career path if they could do it over. Many of the nation's leaders are opting to become free agents. More than 16 percent of the workforce, 25 million people, are self-employed or independent contractors who have opted out of the corporate structure (and the number is growing). Employees resent corporations that monitor e-mail, demand genetic testing, or deny medical coverage based on "pre-existing conditions" like, incredibly, pregnancy.

Several factors make the conventional large corporation archaic: technology obviates the need for layers of middle management; globalization requires the export of jobs; and digital innovation subverts rigid hierarchies. Customers want specialized products tailored to their individual needs; large companies that make standardized goods are losing out in this race. The erstwhile sense of community provided by corporations has also eroded, contributing to a sense of permanent insecurity in the population. The search has begun to replace the steadfast corporate communities of an earlier era: religion, cyberspace, and forms of mass entertainment are all possible alternatives.

The corporation, as an institution, has always commanded center stage in American life despite episodic challenges to excessive corporate power (such as the current Microsoft anti-trust battle). What is new, however, is that many segments of society — including corporate managers and employees — now question the capacity of the corporation to deliver. Citizens in New Jersey and elsewhere are looking for alternatives to conventional corporate structures and they are searching for individual protections as they increasingly become nomads in the work world.

People encounter private power more than government power. Just ask people who are denied health insurance because pregnancy is a pre-existing condition; women who live in breast cancer clusters; people who pay high auto, electric, and property taxes because there is no anti-trust enforcement or checks on development; thousands of middle class managers in New Jersey who have been laid off; people who sit in traffic for hours every day; people who have lost their electronic privacy.

The pace of change in America today is perhaps greater than that of any other industrial period. The Information Revolution makes the Industrial Revolution look slow. In this period, many Americans believe they have lost control of their lives. They have two jobs, a brutal commute, insufficient access to day care and health care, they care for children and parents, they have uncertain jobs and uncertain pensions and they want more control over their existence.

Government, at all levels, has not taken notice of the rapid transformation away from the conventional corporate structure and towards free-agency. The tax code still largely targets employees and imposes heightened burdens, costs and accounting demands on free agents. Health insurance is difficult to obtain for independent contractors and labor laws do not apply to one-sixth of the work force. Only government can redress these needs.

Citizens also need from government the tools to protect their own privacy and security. Their name and identity should never be sold without their permission. Children need protection from corporate marketers who increasingly target children with advertisements and extensions of credit. Citizens should have instant electronic access to the records of people who take care of their most fundamental needs: doctors, nurses, lawyers, insurance companies, banks. Federal rules should make pensions and medical benefits as portable as possible.

As the century ends, there is as much threat to individual privacy from private marketers as there is from government. There have been too many horror stories of HMOs selling medical records to medical device companies, of data entry companies using prison labor to enter the names and addresses of individuals, and of marketers using private information for improper purposes. The country needs greater privacy protections that ensure that an individual's private records are never sold without knowledge and consent. Employees need greater protection so that genetic testing and medical records are kept private. Only then will the concept of privacy embedded in our Constitution become meaningful.

The conventional American corporation will probably never again command the central place in society that it has throughout much of the twentieth century. This profound institutional change means that America has the opportunity to restore the individual citizen, rather than corporate interest groups, to the center of the Republic. The political program that appeals to the citizenry, rather than to special interests, will be the program of the future.

APPENDIX A
FURTHER WRITINGS
BY CARL J. MAYER

Books

Contributing Author, *Lawyers' Desk Book on White Collar Crime* (National Legal Center for the Public Interest, 1992)

Contributing Author, *Collateral Consequences of Convictions of Organizations* (Final Report of the Committee of ABA Section of Criminal Justice, 1991)

Contributing Author, *The United States Constitution: 200 Years of Anti-Federalist, Abolitionist, Feminist, Muckraking, and Progressive Criticism* (New York University Press, 1990)

Co-author, *Public Domain, Private Dominion: A History of Public Mineral Policy in America* (Sierra Club Books, 1985, 340 pp.) (with G. Riley)

Articles

Co-Author, "Coordinating Sanctions for Corporate Misconduct: Civil or Criminal Punishment?" American Criminal L.R. (1992) (with D. Yellen) (33 pp.)

Article, "The Political Economy of Decolonization," *Revue D'Histoire Maghrebine* (1991) (58 pp.)

Article, "Personalizing the Impersonal: Corporations And The Bill of Rights," 41 *Hast. L.J.* 577 (1990)(90 pp.)

Article, "Is Freedom As We Understand It Possible?" 17 *ABA Human Rights Journal,* (Fall/Winter edition 1991).

Comment, "The 1872 Mining Law: Historical Origins of The Discovery Rule," 53 *U.Chi.L.Rev.* 624 (1986).

Numerous articles in the *New York Times, Amicus* (the Journal of the Natural Resources Defense Council), *Newsday, The Denver Post, The Harvard Business Review,* the *Wall Street Journal, The Trenton Times, The Asbury Park Press, The Courier News, The Home News* and *The Newark Star-Ledger.*

APPENDIX B
ACTION ITEMS: HOW TO FIGHT
BACK AGAINST THE SPECIAL
INTERESTS

A. The Environment
Environmental Guide to the Internet - www.govisnt.com
Campus Green Vote - www.cgv.org/cgv
Conservation International - www.conservation.org
Earth Share - www. Earthshare.org
Envirolink Network - www.Envirolink.org
Environmental Defense Fund - www.edf.org
Greenpeace - www.greenpeace.org
Natural Resources Defense Counsel www.nrdc.com
Sierra Club - www. Sierraclub.org

B. Gun Violence
Crime Prevention Coalition 1-800-WEPREVENT
Center To Prevent Handgun violence 202-289-7319
Violence Policy Center - www.vpc.org

C. Fighting Big Tobacco
American Cancer Society — 1-800-ACS-2345
    www.cancer.org.

D. Sprawl
Sprawl-Busters - www.sprawl-busters.com
American Farmland Trust - www.farmland.org
Center on Wisconsin Strategy - www.cows.org/
GreenInfo Network - www.greeninfo.org
Aspen Institute - www.aspeninst.org/rural
American Farmland Trust - 202-659-5170

Sprawlwatch Clearinghouse - www.sprawlwatch.org
Trust for Public Land -
        www.possibility.com/LandTrust/
Rocky Mountain Institute - www.rmi.or
Community Transportation Association of America -
        www.ctaa.org.

E. Lead In the Water

The Clean Water Fund (704)251-0518
Suburban Water Testing 800-433-6595
National Testing Laboratories 800-458-3330

F. Campaign Finance Reform

Public Campaign - www.publicampaign.org/

G. Child Labor

FoulBall campaign - 202-544-7198.
RUGMARK rugs - 212-545-0069.
U.S. Department of Labor -
        www.dol.go/esa//public/nosweat/trends/htm.
Free The Children - 703-534-7045.

H. Fight Back Clearinghouse

Essential Information - www.essential.org

APPENDIX C

IDEAS FOR EMPOWERMENT

THE PRINCETON PACKET

Friday, March 7, 1997

Lower speeds spell victory in truck fight

State posts limits on Route 206

**By Tony Cantu
and James Cho**
Staff Writers

In a victory for Princeton advocates of lowered speed limits, workers Wednesday began installing signs alerting motorists of reductions of 5 to 10 mph along Route 206.

John Dourgarian, a spokesman for the New Jersey Department of Transportation, said all of the signs will be posted by Monday.

The new speed limits cover a wide swath along Route 206, including the area between Province Line Road and Lovers Lane, the lengths between Lovers Lane, Nassau Street, Cleveland Lane and Leigh Avenue, and those portions between Cherry Hill Road and Cherry Valley Road north of the borough.

New, lower speed limits in Montgomery Township also will be posted.

The changes replace speed limits that have been in place for "decades," Mr. Dourgarian said. He added that the new speed limits were six months in the making, and were prompted by concerns from the governing bodies of the township and borough regarding pedestrian safety and increasing truck traffic.

The changes were not based on data showing an exorbitant number of traffic accidents in the affected areas, he said.

"There were concerns about overall safety, not just for trucks but all traffic," he said. "Representatives from the governing bodies asked us to lower the speed limits, and we think it was a reasonable request. They simply were requesting us to slow traffic down to a point that is more manageable."

Princeton Borough Mayor Marvin Reed was among the proponents of lowered speeds. He said his support was based on DOT studies showing traffic increases, as well as concerns from residents in the area over noisy trucks at night when there otherwise was little traffic.

"It's very hard for pedestrians to assert their right to go through crosswalks when cars are going extremely fast," he said. "The second thing that concerned us was trucks. Once they get into the borough's borders, they need to realize they're in an urban area and slow down. In the middle of

Speeds

Continued from Page 1A

the night, cars, and particularly trucks, as they try to speed up to 40 or 45 mph, become quite noisy and bothersome."

Princeton Borough Council member David Goldfarb said the concerns of residents led him to support the changes. "The entire path is primarily residential," he said. "We feel that it is appropriate to have lower speeds where people are living adjacent to the road and crossing the road."

Princeton Township Mayor Michele Tuck-Ponder also was a vocal proponent of the changes.

"I am delighted," she said. "It is not going to resolve all the problems, but it will make it a little bit safer."

Township Committeeman Carl Mayer called the changes "a step in the right direction," but he continues to support even lower limits. He had urged the committee to reduce speed limits along Route 206 in the township to 25 mph.

"I think I've presented the only viable solution and that's a federal ban on long-haul trucks" on Route 206, he said. "The problem that is raining down on Princeton residents is trucks from Canada and the East Coast barreling down on these roads, and they don't belong here. They're just trying to avoid the tolls on the New Jersey Turnpike. The real issue isn't speed limits, but getting the trucks off the road. "

Sandy Solomon, a member of the Princeton Residents Traffic Safety Committee, said the new limits would go a long way toward curtailing truck traffic. She said the citizen group's efforts have garnered support from thousands of residents in the township and the borough.

"We are very pleased at this sign of progress, and grateful to local officials," she said. "We don't think that we should have heavy long-haul trucks on our road."

Township and borough motorists will be eased into the new changes, said representatives of both police departments.

207

Sherry Sylvester

The big truck war

I wonder if Carl Mayer, one of the guys running for Dick Zimmer's congressional seat, has any chance of winning?

Mayer is not only a Democrat, he's a Princeton Democrat, a member of the township committee, which means he would have a particularly difficult row to hoe to get to represent New Jersey's 12th district, which includes Hunterdon County and parts of Mercer, Somerset and Monmouth counties, in Congress.

Which is too bad because Mayer launched a campaign initiative this week that ought to be able to get him elected to just about anything in New Jersey.

Standing in the rain at a truck stop on Route 31, Mayer pledged to fight for federal legislation that would "ban long-haul trucks from local roads unless they show a delivery manifest."

"Massive long-haul tractor-trailers have no place on the local roads of central New Jersey," Mayer said. "They create noise problems, traffic problems and have been involved in serious accidents."

"Who owns Central New Jersey?" Mayer asked. "The trucking companies or the citizens..."

Good question.

Just look at the big-truck coddlers who are proposing the Garden State adopt a policy to woo truckers off the local roads by giving them a break on New Jersey Turnpike tolls.

Not to mention the folks who are constantly berating Central Jerseyites to tear up a big hunk of open space to build truck stops for the poor, tired truckers who persist in parking their big rigs on the interstate shoulders even though folks tend to run into them and get killed.

I'm sure truckers feel bad about smashing a few folks to pieces, but their official position is that it's not their problem.

Last year, in response to victims' families protesting the 55,756 people who have been killed by trucks during the last decade, John Collins, senior vice president of government affairs for the American Trucking Association, said that "truckers should not be targeted when their figures show two thirds of the accidents aren't truckers' fault."

Yeah, right.

What they mean by that is if they're flying along Route 1 in a gazillion-ton truck at 55 miles an hour (which is a charitable estimate) and a van full of kids pulls out and they run them over, they don't accept the blame. The kids shouldn't have been there.

Those 55,756 lives are the cost of doing much more business than we need to by big trucks in this country.

Last year New Jersey Sen. Frank Lautenberg promised to press for tougher rules for big trucks, but so far he hasn't had much luck. The National Transportation Safety Board says that fatigue is a factor in up to 40 percent of all big-truck accidents and they want tougher rules, but even with the regulations, truckers are notorious for forging their documents.

Unsafe and overweight vehicles are often as dangerous a problem as sleepy drivers. Mayer told me that in a recent safety check of trucks going through Princeton, almost 75 percent had safety violations. And when a truck crashes into you, you're usually dead, while truck drivers frequently walk away.

It's hard to figure out why the U.S. Environmental Protection Agency, the Clean Air Act folks and New Jersey's Department of Transportation aren't doing more to get big trucks off the road.

Those folks have spent millions of taxpayer dollars in the last few years in a largely unsuccessful effort to get people to car pool, ride bikes or just stay home rather than pollute the air with their cars. But they seem to have nothing to say about big trucks that pollute lots more than cars, particularly new clean cars.

Their transportation experts say that New Jersey could bring our air into national compliance standards if commuters would only intermittently change their driving patterns by using HOV lanes or telecommuting once in a while.

If that's true, think how clean we could make the air if we took some aggressive steps to get all unnecessary truck traffic off New Jersey roads.

In 1994, Don Phillips reported in the Washington Post that smart companies were transferring more and more freight to rail because it's cheaper and more predictable than trucking. At that time, the American Trucking Association predicted they wouldn't be able to keep up with the trains.

But the truckers have managed to ward off the competition from freight trains, probably by putting Collins' "governmental affairs" department to work lobbying at both the state and federal levels to make sure that nobody undercuts the dangerous and polluting big trucking business.

Another thing that people like Collins do is hand out hefty congressional campaign contributions, which is why it is hard to hold out much hope for Carl Mayer.

Still, the guy's hit on a great campaign platform idea. Hope he doesn't get run down by a big truck.

Sherry Sylvester is a political writer who lives in Somerset County.

where they tried to land as close to

Courier News May 19

Democrat raps ATM 'gouging'

By CHRISTINE SOKOLOSKI
Courier-News Staff Writer

Democratic congressional candidate Carl Mayer has called for federal legislation to put a halt on burgeoning automated bank machine charges.

Mayer criticized automated teller machine — ATM — networks and banks for double-charging users, calling it "unconscionable gouging of ordinary customers."

On April 1, Plus, a computerized national electronic payment network, lifted its ban on ATM operators from charging an access fee to use the Plus network. Other networks soon followed suit.

Consumers are charged by their own bank for using another bank's ATM, and that ATM also can charge the consumer for its use.

Mayer said he supports the ATM Fee Disclosure Act of 1996, an amendment to the Electronic Funds Transfer Act, which would require ATMs to list all charges that a potential transaction would involve before that transaction takes place.

"We are proposing two things," Mayer said, "a federal law that requires disclosure on the screen of exactly how much the transaction will cost you and a ban on surcharges for ATMs."

He also supports congressional legislation that would prohibit a surcharge for ATM use.

"These electronic systems are highly integrated, as well as highly profitable," he said Friday at a press conference at First Union Bank in Lawrenceville. "There is no justification for being charged by any bank beside the one that issued the card to the consumer."

Mayer said he has not had any response from the banking industry but hopes "they will join us, benefiting New Jersey consumers."

Mayer, David DelVecchio and Rush Holt are seeking the Democratic nomination in the June 4 primary for the 12th Congressional District seat. The district includes all of Hunterdon County; Bedminster, Bernardsville, Branchburg, Far Hills, Montgomery, Peapack-Gladstone and Rocky Hill in Somerset County; and parts of Middlesex and Monmouth counties.

The Princeton Packet   Tuesday, May 20, 1997

Mayer seeks help in fight with utility

Township official opposes PSE&G deal

By Tony Cantu
Staff Writer

Princeton Township Committee member Carl Mayer is trying to form a coalition to challenge a settlement allowing PSE&G to pass the costs of closing its Salem II nuclear plant to consumers.

A settlement reached in October 1996 between PSE&G and the New Jersey Ratepayer Advocate, a consumer group, will allow the utility to bill its customers for fixing cracks found at Salem II when the reactor was closed for repairs in June 1995.

The agreement allows PSE&G to continue charging its consumers as if the plant were still operating, rather than trying to find alternative energy sources that could prove cheaper.

In December, PSE&G received permission from the state Board of Public Utilities to recoup the $200 million needed for repairs from its customers.

The average PSE&G customer pays 10 cents per kilowatt hour for electricity, or about $75 a month based on the average use of 750 kilowatt hours per month. Regulators allowed PSE&G to continue charging that rate until December 1999 in order to recoup costs associated with the shutdown.

The Salem plant began operating two decades ago, when PSE&G and Atlantic Electric invested $2.3 billion to build the plant and a precursor, Salem I.

When regulators ordered the power plant be closed for repairs, utility officials at PSE&G and Atlantic Energy discovered that the reactor's steam generator tubes — which carry radioactive water throughout the plant — were cracking.

"What I've done is written to various municipalities to form a coalition of municipalities in Mercer and Middlesex counties," Mr. Mayer said. He said he has received a positive response from South Brunswick Township officials, but declined to name other municipalities that have responded to his calls for a coalition.

"I'm in the early stages of forming a coalition, so no one, including Princeton, has written an ordinance or hired an attorney to intervene," Mr. Mayer said.

Mr. Mayer said he is keeping a close eye on Monroe Township, which is exploring the possibility of buying energy from other sources. If Monroe is successful, he said he plans to introduce the idea to the Princeton Township Committee.

"The technology and the state regulations exist where you could buy energy independently, and not have to be at the mercy of PSE&G," Mr. Mayer said. "We don't have to rely on a monopoly anymore. And we certainly shouldn't be paying for nuclear plant shutdowns."

Once the coalition is formed, Mr. Mayer said a lawsuit will be filed to prevent the rate hike from being implemented.

Mr. Mayer said he is particularly interested in protecting the rights of senior citizens in forming the coalition.

"It's an issue for senior citizens," he said. "These people are on fixed incomes and it's a problem."

Mr. Mayer is working closely with several watchdog groups involved in the issue, including the New Jersey Public Interest Research Group, NJ Citizen Action, the Coalition for Competitive Energy and the Coalition for Fair Competition.

William Potter, a Princeton-based attorney, recently filed two appeals against the rate hike decision on behalf of the Coalition for Competitive Energy, a group composed of industrial users, and the Coalition for Fair Competition, which comprises energy service companies. The latter group includes air conditioning and heating technicians, who argue that PSE&G has an unfair advantage over them.

Mr. Potter was unavailable for comment. An assistant said Mr. Potter filed the appeals on Feb. 24 and that no responses have been received from regulators.

Princeton Township Mayor Michele Tuck-Ponder declined comment about Mr. Mayer's efforts.

"This is something he's taken on as an individual, and I just don't know enough about it," she said. "As a knee-jerk reaction, I can't say whatever the monster utility company is doing is wrong. I need to be more informed before forming an opinion."

Inquirer Magazine

MARCH 16, 1997   THE PHILADELPHIA INQUIRER

The schmooze
EXPRESS

As the frozen New Jersey landscape rolls past the window of his train car, George Zoffinger, a potential Democratic candidate for governor of the Garden State, is looking for a little free publicity.

"If I kiss George Spadoro on the lips, will you take my picture?" he hollers at an Associated Press photographer, as he drapes his arm over the shoulders of Spadoro, a lawyer and former state legislator. Then, his voice rising to carry to the far reaches of the noisy car, Zoffinger, a former state commerce commissioner, announces: "Hey, Zoffinger just kissed Spadoro on the lips!"

In addition to phony smooches, Zoffinger offers real candy bars. He's handing out foil-wrapped "George Bars" that promise "fewer nuts than a Whitman sampler, less fat than the Whitman budget."

"Want a bar?" asks Zoffinger. "We gave two of these to one guy, and he's been in the bathroom ever since." A crowd of men and women gathers around Zoffinger. They laugh loudly.

It's only 240 miles from Newark to Washington, D.C., so why does the trip aboard the Lobby Limited seem to take forever?

Eighteen cars of lobbyists, politicians and bureaucrats, propelled by tradition and free liquor, the ride known officially as the New Jersey Chamber of Commerce train combines all the best elements of a legislative junket and a fraternity party.

This year, the ritual February trip gathered nearly 2,000 of the state's business and political establishment, led by Gov. Whitman, for the four-hour

ride to Washington followed by a dinner to honor the state's congressional delegation. As always, political and business ambitions were played out in a theatrical atmosphere of bipartisan bonhomie.

Over the years, the trip has become a form of political vaudeville where the jokes are dumb, the laughter is loud. However reluctantly, though, the politicians keep coming. This year, Gov. Whitman, up for re-election, took the chamber ride after a two-year absence, a sure way to announce to the political world that she was running again. The reason most pols make the trip seems to be more a fear of not being seen rather than the possibility of conducting any useful business.

Whitman rarely left her seat near the front of the train, as a stream of lobbyists, political operatives and reporters fought their way through the crowds to have a word with her. While she waited for the masses to

come to her, her husband, John, worked the train, at one point reaching out to shake hands with Michael Kalafer, a Flemington auto dealer, who was promoting a plan for a minor league baseball team in Bridgewater. Whitman was soon wearing an obligatory Somerset Patriots baseball cap.

In a nearby car, smaller logjams eddied around State Senate President Donald T. DiFrancesco and Assembly Speaker Jack Collins. But movement ground to a halt altogether in the packed bar cars. There, beefy lobbyists squeezed, sometimes three deep, into the tiny spaces, and began knocking back drinks shortly before noon. In yet another car, John Tomicki, an anti-abortion activist who heads a group called the League of American Families, was cornering lawmakers: "With a stronger family you have less demand for government services and a stronger economy."

The trip, with its drinking, groping and schmoozing, seems straight out of the 1950s — especially to many of the women and younger business people who ride the train.

"It's almost like an anachronism; it's not something you expect for 1997," said Susan Bass Levin, the Cherry Hill mayor and potential candidate for the Democratic gubernatorial nomination. "The whole concept of drinking from 11 o'clock in the morning is very strange to me."

"The train ride has been happening for a long time, and people set time aside," said Levin. "It's like the opening of the opera season in some cities."

Levin, who says she finds the political networking on the train useful, loathes trying to make her way through the crowded bar cars.

"It sometimes seems as if the people who have been in that car have been there for a while," she said. "That, combined with the physical setup, can be very undignified."

"I call it the drunk train to Washington," said Assemblywoman Joann Smith, a Middlesex County Republican, as she took a cigarette break between passenger cars.

Richard McGlynn, general counsel to United Water Co., a North Jersey utility, wondered, "If this train blew up, would New Jersey be better off?"

In one of the bar cars, former State Assemblyman Tommy Foy, now an executive with a nursing-home chain, was drinking and holding court with AFL-CIO lobbyist Bob Yaeckel. Foy gleefully passed out cards saying "complimentary drink" on one side. On the other, the card read, "the bearer is entitled to buy Tommy Foy one free drink."

In another car, a heavyset lobbyist lumbered down the aisle, making his way through crowds of politicians and business people networking their way to Washington.

As he reached a woman in a short skirt and black tights who was seated facing him, he stepped on her foot. Then, he leaned over and put his hand on her knee.

"I'm sorry, dear, did I step on your foot?" he asked, not moving his hand.

"That's OK," the woman replied uncomfortably. "I've got another one."

Women are a relatively recent addition to the Chamber trip. The train ride began as an all-male affair 60 years ago when 50 New Jersey business executives charted a train and traveled to Washington to meet with the state's congressional delegation.

When women started making the trip in the mid-1970s, groping by drunken men was a constant threat.

"I had to spend the entire trip in the restroom," recalls Nancy Becker, a Trenton lobbyist for the cable television industry, who was among the first women to ride the train. She says things have gotten better in recent years, but women still sometimes report being grabbed by male passengers.

"This is practically like a camp meeting compared to what it was like in those days," State Sen. Gordon MacInnes said. "Back then, everyone was pretty liquored up by the time we got to Philadelphia. It was wild and in that sense pretty adolescent."

Even in the current atmosphere, it's hard to believe much serious business gets done, but lobbyists swear there's one giant advantage: The elected officials are a captive audience.

"So when you corner somebody, they can't get away," said Sam Perelli, an anti-tax activist. "You either listen or you jump."

While others were getting drunk, MacInnes, a Democrat, was telling anyone who would listen that Whitman's fiscal policies, particularly her

plan to borrow money to bolster the state pension fund, would be disastrous. "A lot gets done in a very short time," said MacInnes. "You end up connecting face to face with folks that you otherwise don't see for months."

The chamber picks up the cost of most state officials who travel on the train and stay overnight in Washington. The value of the train ticket, hotel room and dinner this year was $500, according to the chamber.

This year, 39 of the 60 legislators on the trip accepted the freebies. The rest paid their expenses out of campaign funds, supplied in large measure by special interests. The cost for Gov. Whitman and her staff was picked up by the Republican State Committee, also funded with special-interest money.

Chamber president Joan Verplanck said the notion of lobbyists peddling influence with elected officials on the trip was overblown.

Verplanck, who has sought to revamp the train trip's image, said a survey of chamber trip passengers found that the majority were there to make contact with other business people, not to corner lawmakers or cabinet officials on legislation.

But in seeking to rehabilitate the trip's image, Verplanck has her work cut out for her. Last year, *60 Minutes* sent Princeton Borough Committeeman Carl Mayer along with a hidden camera. Mayer came back with footage of

some heavy-duty drinking and lobbying for all the nation to see.

"What is going on is that money is buying access to power in ways that ordinary American citizens are shut out," Mayer says. "I think the whole thing should be scrapped."

Here's what you get when you travel on a train with a bunch of people who want to be governor:

Zoffinger's George Bars.

Levin's pink bubble-gum cigars with wrappers proclaiming, "It's a girl."

Suspenders bearing the name of State Sen. Jim McGreevey.

A welcoming party at Washington's Union Station shouting "Andrews for governor," thanks to Rep. Rob Andrews of Camden County.

At the end of it all, there was a dinner to honor the New Jersey congressional delegation. The guest speaker: comedian Al Franken.

The next day, the Chamber of Commerce paid for a return train trip for everyone who wanted one, but many opted for a quicker, quieter plane ride.

"I must confess I flew back the next day with quite a number of other New Jerseyans, and we all stood around at the airport and we all pledged we would never do it again," said Thomas V. O'Neil, a prominent lobbyist and Democratic activist. "And we won't — until next year." □

Critics say money talks aboard schmooze train

By CHRISTOPHER HANN
Courier-News Staff Writer

WASHINGTON — More than 1,300 people from across New Jersey took part Thursday in the annual train trip and dinner sponsored by the state Chamber of Commerce, an event both coveted and criticized for the access it provides to the state's leading policymakers.

Lobbyists, business executives and dozens of public officials used their time aboard a congested Amtrak charter to Washington to

Inside/A-9

■ Whitman uses train ride to talk transportation

■ Notes from on board

solicit prospective clients, confer over pending legislation and occasionally raise a cocktail or two.

"We use this as an opportunity to talk to our members, to legislators," said James Leonard of Branchburg, the vice president for government relations for the state chamber.

But the chamber's annual trip, an

institution of business and political life in New Jersey, also comes under scrutiny from reform-minded critics. They say the trip illustrates the notion that money buys access to elected officials and, in turn, undue political influence.

On last year's trip, a Princeton Township committeeman named Carl Mayer carried a hidden camera aboard the chamber train. The images he captured were later shown on a "60 Minutes" episode on the relationship between lobbyists and legislators in New Jersey. Mayer said the chamber trip resembles "a cross be-

tween 'Animal House' and 'Let's Make a Deal.'"

"It reinforces the clubbiness of those who have access to power," said Mayer, who did not make the trip this year.

Sen. William Schluter, R-Pennington, chairman of the Joint Legislative Committee on Ethical Standards, did not disagree.

"When they want to pay $25, $100, that's fine," Schluter said, referring to campaign contributors. "But when they start giving $1,000, they recognize that money buys results. Don't let anybody tell you otherwise."

Schluter is the sponsor of legislation pending in the Senate that would reduce campaign contribution limits and place greater restrictions on lobbyists.

It would also legalize initiative and referendum for the purpose of reforming campaign finance laws. It's a thorny issue among legislators because it empowers private citizens to place questions on the ballot, and Schluter acknowledged that the legislation may never make it to the Senate floor.

☐ See SCHMOOZE on Page A-9

THE COURIER-NEWS

FRIDAY, FEBRUARY 7, 1997

SCHMOOZE: 'Anyone can get on'

☐ Continued from Page A-1

Although he opposes initiative and referendum, Schluter said he's willing to make it law if it will bring about campaign financing reform.

Schluter's legislation would still allow lawmakers to accept up to $500 a year for out-of-state travel for legislative purposes. He acknowledged that the chamber paid his bill for Thursday's train ride and dinner, as well as a room at the Sheraton Washington.

"In my opinion, it's not excessive," Schluter said. "It doesn't cross the line of influence, as I see it. I could accept this from the chamber

and still vote against them."

Among legislators, he is not alone. Leonard said the chamber paid for about half of the roughly 50 state legislators who took part in the train ride and dinner, at a cost of about $325 per person. He said the chamber's expenses for the trip will be detailed in reports filed later this month with the state Election Law Enforcement Commission.

Responding to criticism of the trip, Leonard stressed that the event is open to anyone willing to pay the $200 fee for the train ride and dinner. The charge does not cover a room at the hotel.

"Anyone can get on," Leonard said.

"It's all above board and in the open."

Gov. Christie Whitman, who rode the train with several cabinet members, said all their costs were paid for by the state Republican Committee. Asked whether she thought the trip provided participants with access to lawmakers not normally available to private citizens, the governor noted that she and her cabinet regularly conduct public meetings around the state that provide "a lot of ability to access."

"It's a very good opportunity to see one another in a very public way," Whitman said of the chamber trip. "It sets up the ability to exchange information."

Carl J. Mayer

THE NEW YORK TIMES, FRIDAY, FEBRUARY 7, 1997

Political Train Carries On a Tradition

Officials Join Business Leaders and Lobbyists on Washington Trip

By JENNIFER PRESTON

WASHINGTON, Feb. 6 — It was easy to tell that Gov. Christine Todd Whitman and the state's Republican legislative leaders were not too worried about their prospects in the election this November.

They remained seated during most of the four-hour train trip from New Jersey today while Democrats, including five gubernatorial hopefuls, never rested, pushing their way through a clamorous and crowded 18-car chartered Amtrak train to make their case to hundreds of business leaders, lobbyists and fellow politicians.

"The party in power sits down, and the party that's out walks around," said Chuck Haytaian, the state Republican chairman, before erupting into laughter.

Officially known as the New Jersey Chamber of Commerce's salute to the state's Congressional delegation, the event began in 1937, when 51 business leaders traveled to Washington to discuss the issues of the day with the state's members of Congress. Over the years, it has evolved into an annual rite.

Want that pending bill to die in committee? This is the time to mention your concerns.

Frustrated by the impact of some state regulations on your business? Hand the Governor your card and she will pass it on to her chief of staff.

All of that access costs only $350 per passenger, which covers the train ticket as well as the cost of a hotel room and dinner.

"You can open doors, but you can't get anything done here," said John Chiaia, who is general counsel for Recycling Specialists Inc., a company based in Jersey City. "It gives you an opportunity to talk to people who you might otherwise not be able to see."

Ulises Diaz, who works as a lobbyist for the United Water Company, said that he hoped to meet elected officials interested in turning over their municipal water companies to United.

"It is all about networking, meeting people," he said. "Eighty-five percent of it is worthless, but that 15 percent is worth a lot."

With a coming race for governor and with 120 members of the State Legislature up for re-election this year, the train trip is immensely important to the five Democrats vying for the party's nomination in June who made the trip. This was their chance to seek to prove to a captive audience, capable of writing checks for campaign contributions, that they can offer the most formidable challenge to Mrs. Whitman in the fall.

It was impossible for anyone to get past State Senator James E. McGreevey, who is one of those Democratic hopefuls, without him grabbing your hand and saying hello. "It's an opportunity to meet people, see old friends and increase your visibility," he said.

Representative Robert E. Andrews, a Camden County Democrat who is also running for governor, said the train trip was an important part of the state's political culture. "And it's fun," he said.

Susan Bass Levin, the Mayor of Cherry Hill who has also tossed her name into the gubernatorial battle, handed out bubble-gum cigars. "We really do need a change," she said. "As Democrats, we have not done a very good job putting the issues on the table."

Former Gov. Jim Florio, who has not said whether he will seek the Democratic nomination, did not board the train, but he did appear tonight at the chamber's annual dinner.

Car No. 8 was the center of power. That is where Governor Whitman and her top aides, along with Republican legislative leaders, held court. As a candidate in 1993, she did walk the length of the train, or "walk to Washington," as the politicians like to call it. But as an incumbent governor, she did not have to worry about reaching out to anyone today. They all came to her.

"Everyone who is serious about running is here," she said. "And I'm running."

There was one elected official, however, who did not make this year's trip. Carl J. Mayer, a Princeton Township committeeman boarded the train last year, accompanied by a cameraman from the CBS News program "60 Minutes." Wearing a hidden camera, the cameraman recorded Mr. Mayer's conversations with lobbyists and business leaders interested in doing business in his town. A segment was run a few months later raising questions about all the influence-peddling on the train.

But Joan Verplanck, president of the Chamber of Commerce, scoffed at the television report and said it did not lead to a reduction in attendance this year. "This event has a life of its own," she said.

Not every Republican was completely happy about sitting on the train today. Former Representative Richard A. Zimmer, who was defeated last year by Robert G. Torricelli in the Senate race, was in a single seat, reading a newspaper. "This is the first year that I have sat," said Mr. Zimmer, who boarded his first chamber train in 1979. "It used to be a point of pride to walk from one end of the train to the other."

The Courier-News

SOMERSET

SATURDAY, MAY 4, 1996

House candidate decries truck traffic

■ **Democrat Carl Mayer would push legislation to keep tractor-trailers on the highways.**

By CHRISTINE SOKOLOSKI
Courier-News Staff Writer

Democratic congressional candidate Carl Mayer on Friday called for a federal law to prohibit tractor-trailers from leaving interstate highways. Mayer, a Princeton township committeeman, unveiled his proposal Fri-

day in the parking lot of a popular truck stop on Route 31 in Hopewell.

"What's wrong with this picture?" Mayer asked, struggling to be heard over the roar of truck engines. "Families come to Central New Jersey for the quiet, the tranquility, the trees and the single family homes — and the 40-ton trucks barreling down behind them."

Mayer is among three candidates seeking the Democratic nomination for the 12th Congressional District seat held by Rep. Dick Zimmer. The two other Democratic candidates are

Rush Holt of Pennington and Dave DelVecchio of Lambertville.

Mayer spoke about the proposal in the parking lot of Mr. O's Family Restaurant at Routes 31 and 518. As tractor-trailers maneuvered around Mayer and a small group of reporters and campaign workers, the Democratic candidate spoke about how he would rid state roads of tractor-trailers.

"What I'm calling for today is federal legislation that would ban long-haul trucks from local roads unless they show a delivery manifest," he said.

If truckers cannot prove they have a delivery on the road the offending trucking corporation would be fined $500. The violation would also carry a four-point penalty on the driver's commercial license.

"Who owns Central New Jersey? The trucking companies or the citizens of New Jersey?" he said.

Trucks take smaller state roads because of a gap in Interstate 95 between New York City and the Trenton area, he said.

To avoid tolls on the New Jersey Turnpike, truck drivers opt to use

smaller state roads such as Routes 31 and 29 in Hunterdon and Mercer counties, Route 206 in Somerset and Mercer counties, Route 1 in Mercer and Middlesex counties and Route 9 through Monmouth County, Mayer said.

"Massive long-haul tractor-trailers have no place on the local roads of Central New Jersey," he said. "They create noise problems, traffic problems and they have been involved in serious accidents."

"This isn't what people move to the suburbs for," he said.

215

Carl J. Mayer

Princetons join forces to battle bypass, trucks

By Dan J. Szczesny
Staff Writer

In an effort to apply pressure on the state Department of Transportation, the Princeton Township Committee has joined forces with Princeton Borough Council to find ways to alleviate truck traffic on Route 206 and study the possibility of litigation over the proposed Millstone Bypass.

A joint task force also will study DOT plans for widening Route 206 and Route 571 in West Windsor and attempt to involve state and county officials in the task force's transportation strategies.

Princeton Borough Mayor Marvin Reed, who first suggested the task force, said Monday that concern over the DOT's proposed state highway projects prompted the development of the joint group.

"We're talking about a whole network of state highway projects all pointing in our direction, but nothing in the center of Princeton that will relieve our congestion," he said.

In addition to Mr. Reed, members of the task force are Carl Mayer and Phyllis Marchand of the Township Committee and Borough Council members Sandra Starr and Roger Martindell.

Representatives from the Princeton Residents Traffic Safety Committee and the Sensible Transportation Options Partnership (STOP) also have been invited to join the task force.

"The main idea of the task force is to control traffic," said Mr. Mayer. "The most promising avenues of doing that, and what I'll be pressing for, is litigation against the state DOT over the Millstone Bypass."

Mr. Mayer, who suggested that the task force be called the Gridlock Busters, said that he would like other communities such as Plainsboro, Ewing and Lawrenceville, "the whole Route 1 corridor," to become involved in stopping the bypass.

The Millstone Bypass is a proposed, 2.3-mile, two-lane road that would extend from the Amtrak bridge at Wallace Road and Route 571 in West Windsor, along the Millstone River, and over Route 1 to Harrison Street. The bypass would have a spur to Washington Road.

According to DOT officials, the bypass would alleviate congestion on Washington Road and Route 1 by eliminating three traffic lights.

Mr. Martindell said halting the bypass was a priority for the task force.

"All alternatives should be ex-

See **BATTLE**, Page 9A

The Princeton Packet

Continued ➜

Tuesday, November 26, 1996

216

Continued from Page 1A

plored, but ultimately I personally want to focus on what we know we can accomplish," he said. "I think the sooner we define the legal issue and pursue our legal remedies the better. I'd rather start exercising our legal muscles now."

Saying that the "bureaucratic and political process is not responsive or quick enough to provide the relief we need," Mr. Martindell said that contacting the Mercer County Board of Freeholders and petitioning them to not abandon Washington Road is one possible avenue for the task force to pursue.

"If we can persuade the county not to abandon Washington Road then one of the premises the state is using to build the bypass will evaporate," he said.

Mayor Reed said one role of the task force will be to determine who will represent the group in the event of litigation.

"Litigation is always a last priority, but in order to be prepared for that we have to be sure to have adequate legal counsel," he said. "One definite priority for us will be to bring DOT back to the table for further discussions here in Princeton."

Ms. Marchand was less enthusiastic about pursuing litigation.

"Number one, it's costly, but more importantly it not only alienates you from the agencies that you need, but sometimes prevents you from dealing with other issues that are also important," she said. "I'm not saying we shouldn't, but I'm hoping we can work things out over the table."

Reducing truck traffic on Route 206 also will be a priority of the task force, said Ms. Marchand.

"The roads are being damaged by these trucks because the roads were not constructed for that kind of vehicle," she said. "If they used the roads that we pay our tax dollars for, like the Turnpike or Parkway, it would take trucks off Route 206. We have to make (DOT) see that our roadways and communities are not designed for truck traffic."

Mr. Mayer, however, proposed federal or state legislation to try to ban trucks from Route 206.

"Unless the truck has a delivery manifest for central New Jersey, I would try to convince state legislators to push for an outright ban," he said. "Most trucks are just driving through from Maine to Florida and using us as an interstate."

According to John Dourgarian, a spokesman for DOT, an origin and destination study of truck traffic on Route 206 will be released "in early December."

"We did 12 consecutive hours surveying large percentages of the total truck traffic on Route 206," he said. "The survey will help us find out where the trucks originate, where they are going, what they are carrying and why the drivers are using Route 206."

Mr. Dourgarian said that DOT has lowered speed limits on several stretches of Route 206 "as part of our ongoing effort to take actions that the community felt would help detour truck traffic."

"Speed restrictions, coupled with a state police truck safety inspection plan, along with working with the N.J. Turnpike Authority to enhance the desirability of the Turnpike as a major through corridor for traffic, will take trucks off community roads," he said. "Our work with the Turnpike Authority includes avoiding toll increases and ensuring that truckers have safe, clean facilities to use."

Some of the new speed limit zones, which will be posted early next year, include:
■ Lovers Lane to the Princeton Borough-Township line at Leigh Avenue will include four speed zones varying from 25 mph to 35 mph.
■ Leigh Avenue to the Montgomery border will have three speed limit zones varying from 30 to 40 mph.
■ Cherry Valley Road to the Hillsborough border will include four zones varying from 40 to 50 mph.

Mr. Martindell said that a "number" of task force members will meet this week to discuss how often the group will convene and whether meetings will be open to the public.

"Some clearly will not be public because they will involve legal strategy, but some may be," he said.

Ms. Marchand suggested that the task force meet at least once a month.

"It's a wonderful idea because it means that there will be a continuity and consistency in the Princetons' efforts to control traffic," she said. "We'll be able to serve as liaisons to our governing bodies as well as to the community."

Carl J. Mayer

THE **PRINCETON PACKET**

Founded in 1786
Bernard Kilgore, Publisher 1955-1967

Tuesday, November 12, 1996

Citizens defeated special interests

To the editor:

I want to thank all the dedicated citizens of Mercer County who worked so hard to prevent the construction of a dangerous and expensive incinerator in our midst. When the freeholders finally voted to kill the project late last week, a great victory was achieved. Democracy and citizen participation triumphed over the special interests. I hope that in the coming weeks the newspapers will reflect upon the truly heroic efforts of citizens from our area who took on the lobbyists and won against overwhelming odds.

While hundreds contributed to the effort, consider the amazing contributions of just a few. When I first began working against the incinerator in 1988, Mary Penney had already been long involved in this 15-year battle. She toiled long hours for no pay despite the obligations of a full-time job and a family. Equally dedicated to the battle was Carol Royal, a Princeton resident whose house became a virtual full-time headquarters for incinerator opponents. Jensine Christensen and Nick Mollis meticulously researched the adverse health effects of incineration and never gave up year after year.

These citizens and others prevailed against a fearsome display of corporate power. The company proposing to build the incinerator — Ogden Martin — contributed handsomely to grease the political wheels. Lawyers and investments bankers were paid millions of our tax dollars to lobby overtime for a project that was flawed from the beginning. A slick public relations firm was hired to convince citizens that they should support the project. Through it all, the opinions of hardworking citizens were held up to ridicule and derision.

Most of the time in politics the special interests triumph over the larger interests of informed citizens. This partly explains the continuing low turnout in American elections. This week in Mercer County, however, years of dedication showed that every so often justice prevails over mercantile greed.

Future observers of our society will recognize that incinerators in the 1990s came to be regarded as nuclear power plants were in the 1970s — obsolete and dangerous technologies. There hasn't been a new order for a nuclear plant in this country since the mid-1970s. Incineration projects are now being canceled wholesale across the land. Mercer County was just the latest project to terminate.

The best and the brightest in the country did not lead the fight against nuclear plants or incinerators. That was left to the those with the least time and money, but the most courage: citizens. I am convinced that the office of citizen is the highest in the land. Certainly our neighborhoods and communities are safer because of dedicated citizens like those who prevailed here in Mercer County.

Carl J. Mayer
Committeeman
Princeton Township

218

THE PRINCETON PACKET

Friday, November 8, 1996

Incinerator project dies in a slow burn

Freeholders trash plan, each other, in 4-3 vote

By Lisa Pevtzow
Staff Writer

After 15 years on the Mercer County front burner, the $260 million Duck Island incinerator project was effectively killed Thursday night.

As dozens of incineration foes whooped and hollered and spontaneously gave the county freeholders a standing ovation, the county board voted 4-3 to reject an ordinance to amend the county's solid waste management plan, y forcing the county administration to scrap the project.

"A miracle in Mercer County," pronounced Princeton Township Committeeman Carl Mayer, one of more than 100 people who packed the freeholder board's meeting room in Trenton awaiting the final vote. "What did it was the resolve of citizens who showed that democracy can beat special interests. This is a huge thing."

With a huge smile on his face, Princeton Borough Councilman David Goldfarb, who worked to help kill the project, described himself as "relieved."

He also said that without the intervention of the two Princetons, which legally forced the county to amend its solid waste plan and hold a round of public hearings, the incinerator most likely wouldn't have gone down in flames Thursday night.

"I don't think this would have happened if (the Princetons) didn't bring the lawsuit," said Mr. Goldfarb. "It took the hearing to turn it around."

The vote, which was split along partisan lines, came at the end of an angry two-hour verbal brawl between the four Democratic and three Republican freeholders. They accused each other of lying, hypocrisy and playing fast and loose with taxpayer dollars.

But by the time the freeholders filed into the room, it was a foregone conclusion to pretty much everyone in the audience — and to them — that the incinerator project was doomed. One person even brought a single black rose in full bloom to bestow on county officials supporting the incinerator.

Freeholder James McManimon, the Democratic swing vote who had been keeping his decision a closely guarded secret, said, "It has eaten away at my gut."

He called County Executive Robert Prunetti, a Republican, "misguided" and blinded by his passions or political affiliation to support the project through thick and thin.

"But this project doesn't make sense any more and if he won't say no, I will," said Mr. McManimon, reading carefully from a prepared statement, which he wanted to be entered into the record.

He said the project was financial risky and three times larger than what the county required to dispose of its garbage. He questioned the county's assertion that its contracts with power utilities were in order and said that the county shouldn't foot 80 percent of the bill for a privately owned incinerator.

"We don't need an oversized, over-priced potentially risky incinerator sitting next to us," he said. "It's the money that has been spent on this project that will cause the taxes to go up," referring to Mr. Prunetti's assertion that voting down the incinerator will force taxes higher.

Freeholder Ann Cannon, the oth-

Continued on Next Page→

219

er board member whose support had wavered, said she could not support the project with Ogden Martin Systems of Mercer County.

"I have not caved in. I have not given into pressure by the party," she said. "At this point, financially, it doesn't make sense. Five incinerators are going under (in the state). Their bond ratings are reduced. Why should we follow?"

The three Republicans freeholders— two of whom were voted out of office on Tuesday — fumed at the Democrats.

"Both of you have cost the taxpayers millions of dollars," charged

Freeholder Michael Angarone, one of the two who lost his bid for re-election Tuesday, of Mr. McManimon and Ms. Cannon. "If this board was going to kill it, they have should have done so before this."

Getting a dig in at Mr. McManimon, he suggested that the Democrat waited until after Election Day to use the results of the two freeholder races as an impromptu referendum.

He also called for the minutes of all the freeholders' executive sessions to be made public, charging that Ms. Cannon and Mr. McManimon said one thing in private and then turned around to declare something entirely different in public.

"Obviously people's words don't

mean too much anymore," said Mr. Angarone, who sat through the meeting furiously pulling on a rubber band and aiming it at the Democrats. "To the freeholder board of 1997 and beyond, God bless you. I hope you come up with a solution for garbage. I have seen none."

Freeholder Joseph Constance, who supported the project and lost his seat Tuesday, warned that if the project fails, "taxes are going to increase, jobs will be lost and the garbage will still be here."

County Executive Prunetti, who had long supported the project, recommended that the freeholders support the project. But if not, he suggested that they abandon the project as quickly as possible and work out a

scenario for repaying $50 million the county already spent on the project.

To cover the debt, the county should add a surcharge of about $40 per ton to garbage tipping fees for the next two years until trash flow control is deregulated and municipalities don't have to dispose of their garbage through the county's plan, he said. After that, Mr. Prunetti suggested, the county should get the state to assume the "stranded investment" burden.

He also warned of an "immediate and definite" tax increase.

To Mr. McManimon, he said, "I think you've had your fill with me and you've done it all the way along ... Please don't blame me for my God-given right to believe in something."

Coalition taps sentiment against water rate hike

By Laurie Lynn Strasser
Staff Writer

The Princetons, Plainsboro and West Windsor are joining forces to fight the largest potential rate increase in the 142-year history of Elizabethtown Water Co.

The proposed 30 percent hike would affect individual customers and fire hydrant service in Princeton Borough, Princeton Township, Plainsboro, West Windsor, Montgomery and 53 other municipalities. Hydrant service is financed either by fire taxes or municipal taxes.

The Princeton Borough Council Tuesday night agreed to join the Princeton Township Committee and any other willing municipal governments to hire the Princeton-based law firm of Potter and Dickinson for $2,500 per municipality to challenge the fairness of the increase before the state Board of Public Utilities.

Princeton Township Committeeman Carl Mayer proposed hiring the law firm in January.

Elizabethtown has 4,610 customers in Princeton Township, 2,427 in Princeton Borough, 5,208 in West Windsor, 3,145 in Plainsboro, 1,727 in Montgomery, and none in Rocky Hill, spokeswoman Donna Yukob said.

If the BPU approves the rate increase, individual customers would pay a total of $416,000 more per year in West Windsor, $332,000 in Princeton Township, $218,000 in Plainsboro, $193,000 in Princeton Borough and $115,000 in Montgomery.

The average annual cost of fire hydrant service would increase about $158,000 in West Windsor, $102,000 in Princeton Township, $71,000 in Montgomery, $58,000 in Plainsboro and $30,000 in Princeton Borough, according to information provided by Elizabethtown and municipal officials.

When R. William Potter, an attorney with Potter and Dickinson, fought a rate hike sought by Elizabethtown in 1989, the water company increased the cost of hydrant service 20 percent rather than the 30 percent proposed and hiked the cost to individual customers 12 percent — compared with the 17 percent proposed.

Elizabethtown raised its rates 8.2 percent in 1991, 4.9 percent in 1992, 5.65 percent in 1993 and 5.34 percent in 1995, said Ms. Yukob.

If the rate hike is approved, the cost of 10,000 cubic feet of water per year would rise from $220.52 to $291.77.

Of 58 municipalities affected by the rate hike, only a few have responded to the Potter firm's proposal to champion their cause, Princeton Township Clerk Pat Schuss said Tuesday.

Plainsboro plans to discuss whether to engage Potter and Dickinson at its meeting Wednesday, said Mayor Peter Cantu, voicing reservations about whether enough towns would band together to absorb an estimated

See **RATE**, Page 9A

Continued ➔

The Princeton Packet

Friday, February 9, 1996

221

Continued from Page 1A

$50,000 to $100,000 in legal fees. He was unsure whether it is worthwhile to stake so much money for an uncertain payoff.

The BPU will hold a public hearing on the rate increase March 7 at the Westfield Municipal Building, Ms. Yukob said. Evidentiary hearings will take place March 27-29, April 15-19 and April 25-26 and April 30, she said.

Of $31.6 million in revenue the rate hike would generate, $22.9 million would help finance a $100 million treatment plant on Canal Road in Franklin Township, the largest, costliest project the utility has undertaken.

The new plant, which relies on surface water, is needed because polluted wells have become too costly a water source and because residential development has increased demand, Elizabethtown representatives claim.

The state Division of the Ratepayer Advocate, a branch of the BPU that is supposed to challenge the increase at the hearings, is "giving away the candy store" because it already has agreed to the need for a plant and its projected cost, Princeton Borough Councilwoman Mildred Trotman said Tuesday.

Borough Councilman David Goldfarb said he was concerned that the real decision-making process is more "political" than "analytical."

"Is it built to accommodate future growth," he asked. "If it is, we shouldn't have to pay for it now."

The plant, which would handle 40 million gallons per day at the outset, has potential to process 200 million gallons per day in the future.

The Princetons, Plainsboro and West Windsor rely almost exclusively on Elizabethtown water. However, only about 30 percent of Montgomery properties, mainly businesses along the Route 206 corridor, draw water from Elizabethtown, rather than wells, said Montgomery Sanitarian Jim Schmidt.

Many of the Montgomery residents who use public water live in townhouses and apartments off Blue Spring Road, Committeeman Ted Maciag said. Because of its high water table, Montgomery has fewer hydrants than surrounding towns, he added.

The Princeton Packet
Tuesday, November 26, 1996

Photo by Alix Nyberg

New Jersey Public Interest Research Group activists gathered in Palmer Square Saturday to protest a PSE&G proposal regarding the Salem nuclear reactors. Princeton Township Committeeman Carl Mayer (left), who joined the protesters, said the proposal is unfair to ratepayers.

NJPIRG cries foul on bailout

By Alix Nyberg
Special Writer

Utility rate hike topic of protest in Square

With colored paper feathers and informational leaflets fluttering in the wind, New Jersey Public Interest Research Group activists wheeled a 6-foot-high plywood turkey into Palmer Square Saturday to protest a PSE&G proposal regarding the Salem nuclear reactors that they say will harm consumers.

"It's a turkey of a deal," the slogan ran, claiming that further investment into the currently inoperable reactors will "gobble up" ratepayers' funds, yet offer no guarantee of improved future service.

PSE&G and Atlantic Electric reached an agreement with the New Jersey Ratepayer Advocate in October that would allow the utilities to charge customers a portion of the costs to repair cracks in the reactors. The Board of Public Utilities could vote on the proposal as early as Monday, Dec. 2, accordingly to Bill Poller of Coalition for Competitive Energy.

Carl Mayer, Princeton Township Committeeman, announced to the strolling crowd that he would urge the Princeton Township Committee and Princeton Borough Council to take legal action against the utilities companies if the measure passes.

"It seems as if the Public Advocate is working for the ratemakers rather than the ratepayers," he said. "It's the shareholders, not the consumers, who should be paying for the reactors."

On Saturday, two days before the Board of Public Utilities' open hearing on the proposal, few local residents broke their stride along Nassau Street to join the consumer activists.

NJPIRG organizers said the turkey has drawn crowds of about 20 people in the other New Jersey towns they have visited in the past two weeks. They said they planned to ruffle feathers with their creation at the public hearing on Monday,

223

Carl J. Mayer

PRINCETON METRO
water rate hike challenge
Princeton Twp. joins

by KATHY HENNESSY
Staff Writer

PRINCETON TOWNSHIP — The township has joined 10 other municipalities in challenging the 30 percent water rate increase proposed recently by the Elizabethtown Water Co.

Last week, township committee members unanimously approved spending $4,000, its share of the cost of hiring Analytic Resources Inc. to represent them in their protest of the rate hike.

The township will go a step far-ther, hiring an attorney to see if it can reduce water rates, according to the committee's resolution.

The water company has said the higher rates would bring in an additional $31.6 million in revenues. Much of the additional revenues would be used to finance and operate a new water treatment plant being built in Franklin Township, Somerset County.

Township engineer Robert Kiser said the 30 percent rate hike is the highest Elizabethtown has ever proposed.

"We have opposed rate hikes three times before, but it's never been this high before," said Kiser.

In the past, the rate hikes have been about 12 to 13 percent, said township attorney Ed Schmierer. Over the past three years, Analytic Resources has been able to reduce proposed rate increases by an average of 3 percent, said Schmierer.

While all members of the committee agreed the township should fight the rate hikes, Committeeman Carl Mayer suggested the town should hire an outside attorney to find additional savings.

"I don't think the savings in the past have been that substantial. I propose we talk to another specialist in the area to see if we could find greater savings," he said.

MAYER QUESTIONED whether it is legal for the company to charge customers for its plant expansion and said he wants to look into other issues such as pollution control.

Under the proposed increase, a township resident who uses 2,800 cubic feet of water or approximately 21,000 gallons of water each quarter — the township average — would pay about $20 more. Currently, the average water rate bill is about $250 a year, said Kiser.

Approval of the state Board of Public Utilities is needed before rate changes can be put into effect.

Elizabethtown Water Co. has said

the new water treatment plant is being built to supplement its Bridgewater facility, providing an additional 40 million gallon daily capacity. The old plant can no longer operate at its 150 million to 160 million gallon daily capacity due to environmental rules, said water company officials. Together, the two plants will provide about 130 million gallons per day.

Water company officials also said they will use the additional revenues to pay for operating and maintenance costs.

On Thursday night, Committeewoman Phyllis Marchand urged the

members of the governing body to consider joining the other towns in the appeal and also hiring an outside counsel.

"I think we should do both. It would not be in our interest not to join the coalition with other municipalities. We would be upset if others didn't join us on other issues such as Route 206 and the airport," said Marchand.

The other towns that have already joined the appeal are Branchburg, Peapack, Gladstone, Scotch Plains, Readington, Linden, Plainsboro, Raritan, South Brunswick and Princeton Borough.

The Times
TUESDAY, JANUARY 16, 1996

224

The Princeton Packet

Tuesday, May 14, 1996

Staff photo by Mark Czajkowski

Princeton Township Committeeman Carl Mayer discusses his opposition to junkets such as the League of Municipalities Convention in Atlantic City during Sunday's appearance on "60 Minutes."

'60 Minutes' of fame

Princeton committeman helps expose 'gravy train'

By Jo Marshall
Staff Writer

Running for Congress involves many challenges, but going undercover for an episode of "60 Minutes" normally isn't one of them.

But Carl Mayer, Princeton Township Committeeman and Democratic candidate for the 12th Congressional District, did just that.

The CBS news program, which aired Sunday night, featured Mr. Mayer with a hidden microphone at the annual New Jersey League of Municipalities convention held in November in Atlantic City.

Officials from every level of government gather at the convention to exchange ideas. But according to Sunday's "60 Minutes" segment, corporations use the convention as a forum to pitch products and win favors from local officials.

"The entire convention really centers around corporations trying to elicit favors from government," Mr. Mayer said Monday. "Convening in Atlantic City to study municipal government is like assembling a religious retreat in Times Square on the problem of virtue."

Many officials there visit corporate booths — laden with lotteries and models to attract their business — rather than attending the educational seminars, he said.

"It's meant to be educational, but why go to Atlantic City to study," he said, noting that one of the state's universities would be a more appropriate location. "It's not an appropriate venue for serious discussions of our nation's problems."

Mr. Mayer said he left the two-day convention with "oodles" of balls, Frisbees, and T-shirts.

Phil Shimkin, producer of "60 Minutes," asked him to do the program last year, following the publication in August of an opinion piece on the previous year's convention by Mr. Mayer in the New York Times. Mr. Mayer referred to the convention as a "taxpayer-financed junket."

"Morley Safer read the article and thought the issue was intriguing," said Kevin Tedesco, spokesman for "60 Minutes."

Mr. Mayer accepted the offer and attended the convention, accompanied by a "60 Minutes" cameraman carrying a hidden camera.

"I don't think CBS would like me to tell you where it was hidden, but it was very small," Mr. Mayer said. "Nobody knew they were being filmed."

Mr. Mayer also was filmed aboard the New Jersey Chamber of Commerce-sponsored annual "gravy train." Aboard the 18-car train that runs from Newark to Washington, about 2,000 public officials schmooze and have drinks with corporate officials.

"It's like a traveling fraternity party," Mr. Mayer said, noting that several reporters asked him why he was taking the train after his outspoken disapproval of it. "I couldn't tell them why, so I said I was doing further research."

Mr. Mayer was not interviewed by Mr. Safer until

See **MINUTES**, Page 12A

mid-February at the CBS studios in New York City.

"He's a very dedicated journalist and asked some very inquisitive questions," Mr. Mayer said.

Noting it was his first time on national television, he said crew members "put a little powder on him" before the interview to make sure he wasn't sweating too much.

On his way through the corridors of CBS he also was surprised by the number of crew members that were familiar with him through editing the program.

"One guy said 'how are you doing' and I asked him if I knew him and he replied, 'you don't know me but I've been editing hours of you eating shrimp,'" he said. "You don't realize how much it takes to film all these pieces."

CBS didn't tell Mr. Mayer until Friday that the show would be aired Sunday but he said it was a nice gift for his mother, who was visiting for Mothers Day.

"They really put together an interesting piece that was reduced from hours and hours of tape," he said. "It was funny and yet it got to the serious point."

Carl J. Mayer

The Princeton Packet

Tuesday, October 3, 1995

Split committee supports 25-mph limit on Route 206

By Steve Janas
Staff Writer

Against the wishes of Mayor Michele Tuck and Committeewoman Phyllis Marchand, Princeton Township Committee members approved a resolution Monday night urging the state to reduce the speed limit on Route 206 throughout the township to 25 mph.

The measure was actually an amendment to another resolution urging the DOT to lower speed limits to the "lowest practical level." A memo from Township Engineer Robert Kiser suggested speeds ranging from 25 mph to 35 mph.

The amendment to request a flat 25 mph speed limit was made by Committeeman Carl Mayer, after several residents demanded action to reduce the number of trucks rumbling through the township.

For several months, residents have complained that truck traffic on the highway has created excessive noise, damaged houses and historic monuments, and endangered residents and other motorists.

In voting against the measure, Mayor Tuck and Ms. Marchand argued that it was unrealistic to expect the DOT to agree to such a low speed limit, and that demanding such a move might be deemed overly confrontational by the DOT.

Mayor Tuck pointed out the state

PMC 'offices' receive reprieve

Princeton Township Committee members unanimously introduced an ordinance Monday night that could delay up to six months a decision on the fate of seven houses owned by the Medical Center of Princeton that are used for non-residential purposes.

According to Township Attorney Edwin Schmierer, the ordinance, for which a public hearing will be held Oct. 16, removes hospitals as facilities permitted in residential zones.

Mr. Schmierer said the ordinance will give the Princeton Regional Planning Board, as well as a zoning subcommittee, a chance to develop more precise regulations on the types of facilities permitted in residential zones.

In response to a change in state laws, the Planning Board is undergoing a comprehensive review of its conditional use ordinances, which govern everything from churches to golf courses in portions of the township and borough zoned for residential use.

The medical center has been operating several houses on Harris Road as offices, among other uses, for at least 10 years. The use has technically been in violation of zoning laws, but the hospital has filed an application with the Planning Board to win approval to continue using the houses as offices.

Monday's action by the committee will obviate the need for any Planning Board action, Mr. Schmierer said.

— Steve Janas

has already agreed to several measures designed to mitigate traffic on the highway, including a speed survey, a traffic count and other studies.

Even Committeeman Steven Frakt, who voted in favor of the resolution, expressed strong reservations.

"You all want 25 mph, we'll put it in," he said. "Maybe you'll get it, maybe you won't. But Princeton residents drive that road, and when they start getting tickets, there will be just as big a crowd in here saying why is it only 25 mph?"

However, several residents, including members of the grassroots Citizens Traffic Safety Committee, said that only by drafting strong resolutions will DOT be prodded into action.

226

Mayer

VIEWPOINTS

The New Gold Rush Despoils The Land and the Treasury

By Carl J. Mayer

A SECOND Gold Rush is gripping the American West. But in this one, unlike in the Gold Rush of 1849, American taxpayers and the environment are paying, dearly. The nation's public lands are being irreparably pillaged for exorbitant private gain, often by foreign corporations. To halt this senseless gold giveaway, Congress and the administration must act immediately.

The current gold rush results from impressive recent advances in gold mining technology — and from soaring gold prices. Novel extraction methods permit corporations to profitably recover deposits of tiny gold flecks, some invisible to the naked eye, otherwise known as microgold or no-see-'um gold.

To do this, large mining conglomerates are de-

Newsday / Gary Viskupic

vouring western lands at an unprecedented rate, constructing mines of titanic proportions. Modern quarries sometimes reach down into the earth several hundred feet and measure almost a mile around their perimeter. Colossal dump trucks cart 10-ton loads of microgold bearing rock to cyanide sprays that leach out the gold. Some pits employ hundreds of people and operate 24 hours a day, seven days a week. Most of these megamines are owned by foreigners, main-

Carl J. Mayer, a professor of law at Hofstra University, is the author of several articles on mining law and of "Public Domain, Private Dominion" (Sierra Club).

ly Australians, Britons, Germans and Japanese.

Almost all of this Promethean-scale mining takes place on public lands — property owned by all Americans. The citizen-owners of this land receive no benefit from the current gold rush, however, because of an outdated 19th-Century statute. Incredibly, the 1872 Mining Law permits anyone to enter public lands, stake a claim, and take valuable minerals — including gold, silver and copper — for free. In theory all 732 million acres of public lands (one-fourth of the country) are open to mining. Yet these lands are supposed to be managed for our benefit by the Interior Department.

The land can be purchased ("patented") outright for as little as $2.50 an acre, about the price of popcorn in a New York City movie theater. Anxious to snap up the nation's biggest bargain, min-

ers are inundating government land offices, filing hundreds of claims per day. Local authorities report shootings that are reminiscent of the Wild West between individuals disputing land rights.

The improbable combination of hypermodern technology and an antiquated law portends environmental disaster. The 1872 Mining Law has no provisions for protecting or rehabilitating mineral land, even though modern mining methods destroy vegetation, erode soil, pollute streams, disrupt aquifers and scar landscapes. The cyanide spray used to mine microgold poisons land and water.

Once abandoned, mining pits fester like sores on our public lands. Nothing prevents corporations from deserting mine sites, and companies often leave behind waste piles, dangerous open pits and caustic pools. (These pools attract migrating birds, many of which die from the cyanide).

Although counseled by the General Accounting Office, the investigative arm of Congress, to require miners to post a bond to insure against environmental damage, the Reagan-Bush Interior Department refused.

The mining law is also a budget buster. The United States is the only nation that gives away its precious minerals. Other countries lease (rather than sell) mineral lands and take at least a one-eighth cut for the government. Estimates place precious mineral production from our public lands at more than $15 billion per year, more than half of it coming from microgold, and none of it going to the U.S. Treasury. In just one example, the Australian-owned Newmont Mining Corp. plans to mine reserves worth $6 billion at current prices; we, the citizen-owners of this precious commodity, will never see a dime of it. Even worse, one government study concluded that the paltry $2.50 fee paid by miners for an acre of land "barely covers expenses of making title on the part of the United States." That study was made in 1880!

Today, the taxpayer loses doubly because lax enforcement of the mining law lets claimants brazenly speculate with public land for illicit private gain. Frequently, acreage is fraudulently patented as mineral land and used not for mines but for resorts, junkyards, shopping centers and, in one instance, a house of prostitution. Often, the federal government turns a blind eye to this outright chicanery. In 1986, for example, the government sold 17,000 acres of public mineral land for $42,500; weeks later, the new owners peddled this same land to the Shell Oil Co. — a British concern — for $34 million. Shell, which admits that it has no plans to mine the land, may be speculating with it.

> *'Lax enforcement of the law lets claimants brazenly speculate with public land for illicit private gain.'*

The mining law remains a barnacled monument to congressional inaction and mining industry power. Since its enactment, five amply funded blue-ribbon congressional commissions have recommended amendment or repeal. Each time, mining corporation lobbyists, spending thousands of dollars, thwarted reform by pressuring key western legislators.

But the days of the infuriating, irrational, indefensible mining law may be numbered. Large-scale corporate mining has mobilized opposition to environmentally dangerous mines throughout the West. For the first time in a decade, Congress plans hearings on replacing the mining law.

Our representatives should immediately replace the current laissez-faire system with environmental regulations on mining and provision for some return for the citizen-owners of America's minerals. Until this is done, corporations will continue to plunder the public commonwealth.

NEWSDAY, TUESDAY, JULY 11, 1989

VIEWPOINTS / 1989

Denver Post Trail E

Foreigners are ripping off our resources

CARL J. MAYER

ALTHOUGH Americans just fought a war to secure petroleum resources halfway around the globe, we're giving away precious mineral resources at home. In the last few years, foreign multinational companies have acquired, for virtually nothing, the nation's most valuable gold deposits. In extracting this bounty, these same foreign conglomerates are ruining the environment of America's most pristine land.

All this is being accomplished under an arcane 19th century law that permits mining on public lands — property collectively owned by all Americans and managed by the federal government. Over 732 million acres of public lands (a fourth of the country) is open to mining.

Incredibly, the law — the 1872 Mining Act — still permits anyone to enter public lands and take valuable minerals free, including gold, silver and copper. The land can be bought outright for as little as $2.50 an acre, about the price of popcorn in a movie theater.

Foreign corporations are exploiting this outdated provision to extract billions of dollars of gold and other minerals from public lands located primarily in the Western states: California, Colorado, Nevada, Oregon, Utah and Wyoming.

This giveaway is so astonishing because these gold resources are owned by you and me: the taxpayer. If the Rockefeller family sells Rockefeller Center to Mitsubishi bank, that may be their business. But if the American government donates the nation's valuable gold deposits — resources held in trust for all the people — to foreign firms, this is decidedly a matter for the American citizenry.

Consider some recent exploits of foreign multinationals:

✔ Newmont Mining Corp. — owned jointly by British and Australians — has opened a gargantuan gold mine on public land in Nevada. This quarry reaches down into the earth the length of a football field; colossal dump trucks cart 200,000-pound loads of gold-bearing rock. While this mine is slated to yield reserves worth $6 billion at current prices, the citizen-owners of this property will receive nothing in return.

✔ Sometimes foreign corporations brazenly speculate with U.S. property. Recently, the government sold 17,000 acres of public mineral land to an unidentified foreign speculator for $42,500; weeks later, the new owners peddled this same land to the British-owned Shell Oil Co. for $34 million. (Shell admits it has no plans to actually mine the land.)

✔ Canadian corporations, like Echo Bay Mines Co. and American Barrack Resources Co., have been gobbling up public acreage. Typical is a large-scale gold mine planned by Noranda Minerals Co. of Canada near Cooke City, Mont. The proposed mine site is within 2 miles of Yellowstone Park and the Absarokee-Beartooth Wilderness. Already, exposed rock at the mine site is leaching poisonous drainage into two adjacent streams, both of which feed into tributaries of the Yellowstone River.

Although modern mining methods pollute streams and scar landscapes, the ancient 1872 Mining Law has no provisions for protecting public land. Nothing prevents foreign corporations from deserting mine sites and leaving behind waste piles, dangerous pits and caustic chemicals like sulfuric acid and cyanide. The mining industry generates twice as much solid waste annually as that carted to industrial and municipal landfills combined; abandoned mines are fast becoming the Superfund sites of the future.

Despite this, the Interior Department remains uninterested in ever, identifying foreign operators on our public lands. Although the Agriculture Department annually publishes a list of foreign owners of U.S. agricultural land, nothing comparable exists for much more valuable mineral land. If a foreigner owns a clump of United States dirt, he has to report it to the world; if the same foreigner acquires our gold, nobody is the wiser. For all we know, foreigners control every dime of public mineral production in America.

There is no reason to xenophobically reject all foreign activity on public lands, but Americans are at least entitled to know whether there is reciprocity. Can American corporations mine free on foreign-owned lands?

Most countries, like Australia and Canada, carefully monitor foreign mining. And every other country in the world assesses some royalty on mineral production; applied here, this would result annually in hundreds of millions of dollars of federal revenue.

Considering that opinion surveys indicate that three-quarters of Americans fear U.S. sovereignty is threatened by foreign investment (which now totals $2 trillion), we should at least know the extent that other nations determine our mineral destiny. Americans were loathe to permit the Yellowstone Park concession to fall into the hands of Matsushita, a Japanese company. And Congress has banned the export of timber, taken from federal lands, to Japan.

Now is the time to plan the fate of our most valuable public mineral resources.

Recently Arkansas Sen. Dale Bumpers and West Virginia Congressman Nick Rahall introduced legislation to repeal the 1872 Mining Law. This would at least loosen the grip of foreign interests on American mineral land.

Write to your congressman to support this effort.

Carl J. Mayer, an assistant professor at Hofstra Law School, testified last fall before the U.S. Congress Subcommittee on Mining and Natural Resources

Denver Post
4/6/91

TOWN TOPICS, PRINCETON, N.J., WEDNESDAY, JULY 12, 1995

County Incinerator Work Should Cease Until Criminal Activity Is Investigated

To the Editor of Town Topics:

There is a bad odor lingering in Mercer County involving the planned Mercer County incinerator. The odor lingers even though the incinerator — which will have enormous consequences for all Mercer residents, including Princeton residents — has yet to be built.

Even though no trash has been burned, something smells fishy about the project because of the way it has been funded.

Taxpayers already know that the Mercer County Improvement Authority has spent tens of millions on consultants and public relations people for a project that has yet to be built. Taxpayers already know that they are footing the bill for this project. And taxpayers already know that many investment banking firms that are major financial contributors to the Republican and Democratic parties in New Jersey have earned millions from this planned project even though not a brick has been laid, and even though there was no competitive bidding for the project.

But what taxpayers don't know is that one of the consultants paid with our money for this project is a criminal organization. That's right: criminal.

The MCIA admits that it hired a firm called Consolidated Financial Management to work on the Mercer Incinerator. The firm was paid handsomely for the work.

The problem is that the owner of this firm, Joseph Salema, pleaded guilty earlier this year in federal court to criminal charges of sharing in kickbacks that were given on municipal bond deals in Camden County. Essentially, Consolidated Financial Management profited at taxpayer expense and received money under the table for working on public projects. As the Judge who accepted Salema's guilty plea indicated: "Sounds like a kickback to me." Salema could face up to ten years in prison. Privately, the firm called its scheme: "A buck a bond."

The problem is this: if there was criminal activity involving municipal bonds in Camden County could there have been criminal activity in Mercer County when the same firm — Consolidated Financial Management — was involved? This is one heck of a question and to date I don't know that any local, state or federal prosecutors have answered it. Nor is it an improbable question. As the United States Attorney said about Consolidated Financial Management: "It would not be fair to assume that this was a one-time deal ... and these problems probably are not confined to this utility authority."

I therefore call on the leaders of the major political parties, journalists, and prosecutors to investigate as to whether any criminal activity took place in connection with Consolidated Financial Management work for the Mercer County Improvement Authority. The MCIA itself should disclose whether it has knowledge of such activity, and it should turn over all documents relating to Consolidated Financial Management to federal and state prosecutors.

Until this question is answered, all work on the Mercer County Incinerator should cease.

CARL J. MAYER
Princeton Township Committeeman
Battle Road

Carl J. Mayer

TOWN TOPICS, PRINCETON, N.J., WEDNESDAY, APRIL 26, 1995

Committeeman Hopes Governing Bodies Can Together Save on Insurance Costs

To the Editor of Town Topics:

At a public meeting on the Township and joint budgets, I may have caused some confusion by speaking frequently about insurance costs. My only goal is to determine whether, through clever purchasing, the Township can save money — for the taxpayer — on its insurance bill.

One thing I don't want to do is give the impression that to save money, the Township should reduce the level of coverage for its valuable employees. To the contrary, my goal is simply to make an effort to obtain the same, or better, level of service at a lower price.

By my calculation, insurance costs may comprise as much as $1 million of the Township budget. This is $1 of every $20 spent. I may be wrong, but I would hope that we can take action to reduce our insurance tab.

What I have suggested we do is the following: review our insurance expenses and see whether we can put out for bid the insurance business of the Township on the open market. Perhaps by doing this we can achieve cost savings.

I want to thank my colleagues on the Township committee for agreeing to pursue this idea. I also want to thank my Borough Council colleagues for listening. And I want to thank Council member Sandra Starr who has already called and shown an interest in jointly pursuing insurance cost saving ideas, and even — in a terrific recommendation — looking into joint purchasing with the School Board.

Whether you are for or against consolidation, I don't think anyone would oppose all these entities getting together to save money on insurance bills.

But my real purpose in writing is to ask the community for help. Not only does Princeton have an enormous wealth of knowledge and talent, but I speak so often with businesspeople, academics, and consultants in the community about their frustration with high taxes and the inability of state and federal government to respond.

Well, here is an opportunity to achieve something concrete right in the neighborhood. We could sure use the help of anyone with knowledge about insurance purchasing. If you have the time and inclination, pick up the phone or drop us a line down at Township Hall.

CARL J. MAYER

Battle Road

230

Friday
December 1,1995

10A

™PRINCETON☙PACKET
Tenacre's generosity should be applauded

To the editor:

Princeton Township has been in the process of acquiring the Poe property (located on the Old Great Road) as an open space site for the entire community.

The township has received state Green Acres money for this acquisition and the township is preparing to commit taxpayer funds for this important project.

At our last meeting I suggested that we explore the possibility of soliciting contributions from the neighbors of the Poe property to reserve this important parcel of land.

To my surprise and delight one of the neighbors — The Tenacre Foundation — generously offered, in short order, to contribute $100,000 toward the cost of acquiring the property.

I have been working to improve the environment and to preserve open space in this region for almost 15 years. The generous act of the Tenacre Foundation is one of the most thoughtful and civic-minded that I have observed.

I hope the generosity of the Tenacre Foundation will inspire other neighbors — as well as other institutions in town — to contribute more to this open space project and others.

All taxpayers in town should also be grateful to the Tenacre Foundation for reducing their tax burden. This type of community spirit and civic-mindedness should be honored.

The Friends of Princeton Open Space should also be recognized for the hard work the group has contributed to open space in this region.

Carl J. Mayer
Committeeman
Princeton Township

Carl J. Mayer

The Princeton Packet

Friday
July 7, 1995

Tax bills require more information

To the editor:

When I ran for Princeton Township Committee last year I promised to work to make the property tax bills that all residents receive in the mail more understandable. I have only partly delivered on that promise. The bills going out to Princeton taxpayers have pie charts that clearly set forth township revenues and expenses.

More is needed, and here is why: without historical comparisons, the taxpayer cannot evaluate the performance of elected officials. An historical comparison in Princeton Township, for example, would reveal that between 1991 and 1995, the municipal budget in Princeton Township increased a whopping 31 percent — an average 7.8 percent per year. This is much more than either the Consumer Price Index (which has averaged about 3 percent per year) and it is much more than the Consumer Price Index for our area, which has averaged only 2.6 percent for the last four years. From 1991 to 1995, tax increases in the township averaged 6.2 percent. Taxpayers have a right to know — in clear fashion — how their elected officials are doing at handling their tax dollars based on historical performance and relevant indexes.

No corporation would dare ask shareholders to fork over dollars without providing an annual report that gives historical data. But this is precisely what most municipalities do and what Princeton Township and other Mercer County towns do. Some municipalities, however, are more forward looking and actually provide not only this data, but a comprehensive annual report. We need that here in Princeton and in Mercer County, where budgets are indecipherable to even the reporters that cover the localities.

If more information were made public, the taxpayers could better judge our performance and make suggestions for saving money. By digging through the budget myself in Princeton, I have found that there are three areas ripe for savings:

1. Insurance costs. These eat up over $1 million a year out of a $20 million budget. Already, because I have suggested changing carriers, our current carrier has agreed to rebates. I hope we can save more money in the future.

2. Consultants. I was amazed to learn that Princeton Township alone spends over $1.1 million per year for 43 different consultants. I bet there are some savings there.

3. Utility bills. They are high and going higher. This is another area for savings. If the budget and tax information the township — and in any town in Mercer — were presented more clearly, taxpayers and citizens could make their own suggestions. There is much more work to do.

No taxation without clarification. If you agree that more information is needed scribble this phrase on the tax bill you are about to pay. If enough taxpayers do this, perhaps the information will follow.

Carl Mayer
Committeeman
Princeton Township

232

THE PRINCETON PACKET

TUESDAY
April 4, 1995

Joint effort could help trim insurance costs

To the editor:

At public meetings on the Princeton Township and joint Princeton budgets, I may have caused some confusion by speaking frequently about insurance costs. My only goal is to determine whether, through clever purchasing, the township can save money — for the taxpayer — on its insurance bill.

One thing I don't want to do is give the impression that, to save money, the township should reduce the level of coverage for its valuable employees. To the contrary, my goal is simply to make an effort to obtain the same, or better, level of service at a lower price.

By my calculation, insurance costs may comprise as much as $1 million of the township budget. This is $1 of every $20 spent. I may be wrong, but I would hope that we can take action to reduce our insurance tab.

What I have suggested we do is the following: review our insurance expenses and see whether we can put out for bid the insurance business of the township on the open market. Perhaps by doing these we can achieve cost savings.

I want to thank my colleagues on the Township Committee for agreeing to pursue this idea. I also want to thank my Borough Council colleagues for listening. And I want to thank Councilwoman Sandra Starr, who has already called and shown an interest in jointly pursuing insurance cost-saving ideas, and even — in a terrific recommendation — looking into joint purchasing with the school board.

Whether you are for or against consolidation, I don't think anyone would oppose all these entities getting together to save money on insurance bills.

But my real purpose in writing is to ask the community for help. Not only does Princeton have an enormous wealth of knowledge and talent, but I speak so often with businesspeople, academics and consultants in the community about their frustration with high taxes and the inability of state and federal government to respond.

Well, here is an opportunity to achieve something concrete right in the neighborhood. We could sure use the help of anyone with knowledge about insurance purchasing. If you have the time and inclination, pick up the phone or drop us a line down at Township Hall.

Carl J. Mayer
Committeeman
Princeton Township

Carl J. Mayer

Corporations gain from tax code

CARL MAYER

This week, while millions of Americans completed their struggle with Byzantine forms and rising tax rates, the chieftains of America's largest corporations will celebrate an increasingly benevolent Tax Code.

With good reason. The tax burden on corporations, particularly large corporations, is declining while it gets tougher for average American families to meet their tax obligations every year.

Consider tax rates. Individuals will pay up to 40 percent of their 1994 income to the federal government. Combined with rising local and state taxes, many citizens will fork over 50 percent of their income to the government. This estimate does not even include user fees: the hidden taxes politicians have been quietly hiking for the last decade. When taxpayers renew their driver's license, or obtain a marriage certificate, or use emergency medical services, they are paying tariffs that have far outraced the inflation rate in recent years.

CORPORATIONS, BY contrast, will only pay 35 percent of their income in federal taxes, making American corporate tax rates among the lowest in the western industrial world. (Many European nations impose a 40 percent corporate tax rate, while Germany, for example, taxes corporations at a 50 percent rate.)

In practice, corporations almost never pay the full tax rate because of plentiful loopholes unavailable to individuals. Companies can deduct rent, repairs, and the infamous "business lunch." Corporations can reincorporate or move overseas to escape tax liability; they can hide assets and it is well-documented that multinational corporations frequently underreport the amount of income earned in the United States.

The non-partisan Tax Foundation, a Washington research group, estimates that when all deductions and loopholes are accounted for, the effective federal corporate income tax rate is only 23 percent. And the percentage of federal receipts attributable to corporate taxes has fallen dramatically since the 1970s (from a high of 17 percent in 1970 to only 9.2 percent in 1993).

Individuals increasingly bear the burden of federal, state and local taxation because special interest lobbyists have jerry-rigged the entire structure to benefit large corporations. These lobbyists daily swarm over Capitol Hill, ramming through special tax treatment for cigarette advertising, for savings and loan operators, and for agribusiness. Each loophole adds another layer of complexity. This intricacy, while benefiting Big Business, has, for individuals, turned the Tax Code into what President Bush's Tax Commissioner calls "a virtually impenetrable maze." Congress has compounded the problem by enacting ten major revisions to the Tax Code since 1981, further diminishing respect for the system and undermining the willingness of even law-abiding taxpayers to properly calculate their tax burden.

WHEN JIMMY CARTER called the Tax Code "a disgrace to the human race," even he didn't realize that corporate loopholes would be expanded and extended. An illuminating example is the $3 billion a year tax break for corporations that operate in the United States Commonwealth of Puerto Rico.

This one provision of the Tax Code, Section 936, allows corporations to take a tax credit for the amount of profit they make in Puerto Rico. Giant American pharmaceutical corporations are the principal beneficiaries of this largesse. The General Accounting Office, the investigative arm of Congress, found that the tax savings of one concern, Pfizer, amounts to about $156,000 per worker or six times the average compensation for workers at Pfizer's Puerto Rican operations. Sadly, this tax dodge, while draining the Treasury, is in no way linked to the number of jobs corporations create for the depressed Puerto Rican economy.

BUT THE GREAT corporate tax loophole machine just keeps on rolling under an administration allegedly committed to change and, in the words of President Clinton, to "breaking the stranglehold ... the lobbyists have on our government." After a multi-year, multi-million dollar lobbying effort, the drug industry convinced the Clinton Administration to retain the preponderance of their Puerto Rican subsidy. No resources were spared in the effort to rescue a corporate tax subsidy: lobbying firms, law firms, former members of Congress and other wheeler-dealers were all enlisted in the battle. And Section 936 is only one example: the Office of Management and Budget estimates that in 1995 taxpayers will lose $53.3 billion in various tax breaks for corporations.

Despite promises from politicians of tax reform, the so-called "Tax Freedom" day for individuals keeps moving back. This means that if the average middle income taxpayers' 1994 salary, starting from January 1, went only to pay taxes, it would have taken until May 3 for that taxpayer to meet all the federal, state and local payments due. By comparison, this Tax Freedom day was March 8 in 1940, and it would have been sometime in April before the 1980s. It also takes longer to comply with the code: Americans will spend an average of 21 hours and 42 minutes to do federal, and state tax returns this year.

Citizens may want to consider — as they spend more time and money each year on tax compliance — demanding that when politicians enact tax laws that they stop coddling the special interests and start elevating the concerns of individuals over the compulsions of powerful corporations.

234

The Times
TUESDAY, MARCH 7, 1995

Residents want action on Rt. 206 truck traffic

By DAVID NEWHOUSE
Staff Writer

PRINCETON TOWNSHIP — The Township Committee wrestled with the big picture of traffic congestion on state Route 206 through Princeton last night, and more than 40 residents were there demanding action.

The committee agreed to ask the state Department of Transportation for a new traffic study, in an effort to win a lower speed limit. The speed limit on Route 206, which is set by the DOT, is 45 mph through much of the township and 40 mph for a shorter stretch.

Residents are pleading for a 30 mph limit from the Montgomery line to the north to Province Line Road to the south. The road in Princeton Borough has a 30 mph limit for most of its length.

Residents have complained about both noise and safety from the growing volume of traffic, especially big 18-wheel tractor-trailers. Township police verified that the accident rate jumped 55 percent between 1991 and 1993 — the last year with complete figures — going from 58 to 90 accidents.

Federal highway construction is the cause, officials agreed — but what is the short-term solution for the state-controlled route?

Officials have made the point over and over that, much as they or residents may dislike it, trucks have the same right to use a federal highway as anyone.

"It's clear that the one thing we can do is to check on speed limits," Committeeman Steven Frakt said. Police Chief Anthony Gaylord said patrols have already been stepped up in the last week or two, and will continue to be.

But Committeeman Carl Mayer pressed for harder and faster action. "I really want us to check for speed, noise, whatever. Let's get the gover-

nor on our side — those trucks rattle right past Drumthwacket."

The committee agreed with Mayer's suggestion that municipal staff investigate every legal option the town has for slowing down traffic.

TOWNSHIP ENGINEER Robert Kiser will ask the DOT to do a safety check of the road, which is some 60 years old and was not built for a fraction of the heavy traffic it now bears. The road is being re-surfaced — but not reconstructed — this spring.

Some officials said it is the safety of the road, especially now that it is thickly settled, that may ultimately

carry the most weight in pressing for a regional by-pass.

Princeton Regional Planning Board Vice Chairman Alain Kornhauser presented a picture of traffic throughout the northeast region as coming all too often through Princeton.

Kornhauser explained that every single trucker who wants to drive from New England to Philadelphia and south now has three choices: they can take Interstate 95 "all the way," including the New Jersey Turnpike; they can take Interstate 287 to Somerville and then Route 202 to I-95, or they can take I-287 to Somerville and then Route 206

through Princeton to I-95.

Kornhauser explained that the travel times for all three routes are identical, and Princeton's route has no tolls. "In a sense, it's a coin toss which way these truckers go," he said.

The toss-up had one simple result, he said: "In some sense, we're looking down the gun of at least a third of that traffic. What can we do about that? We should make it very difficult to go through Princeton."

Some residents have asked the state DOT to endorse an old concept which was dropped years ago — re-routing Route 206 to the west of both Princeton and Lawrenceville.

Carl J. Mayer

The Times

FRIDAY
SEPTEMBER 1, 1995

DOT draws fire for ruling on Rt. 206 bridge limits

By DAVID NEWHOUSE
Staff Writer

PRINCETON TOWNSHIP — Local truck traffic opponents were dealt a blow this week when the Department of Transportation refused to consider a weight limit on the aging Route 206 bridges over Stony Brook. In a letter to township engineer Robert Kiser, the DOT stood by a September 1994 inspection which found the two bridges still able to support trucks weighing 40 tons.

Local activists had pinned their hopes on a weight limit as the quickest way to detour interstate trucking around Princeton.

Last March, a DOT report found that the bridges need major repair. The stone arch bridge built in 1792 is probably the oldest of 6,000 spans in the state highway system, DOT spokesman Jeff Lamm said. It was rated in "fair condition" based on 1990 and 1992 inspections.

Ironically, the 1896 trestle bridge located immediately south is in worse shape. The newer bridge was rated in "poor condition" in 1990 and 1992.

Repair work will be done in the next three to five years, Lamm said.

On July 31, Kiser sent a letter asking the DOT to reinspect the bridges and prove that they are still safe. "I was saying, 'Hey, you're not indicating anything newer (than 1992) here, but during my cursory examination I have found signs that further deterioration has occurred,'" Kiser said. "Looking at the number of trucks that go over it, the structure takes a real pounding."

Interstate trucking in the area has shot up since the completion of Interstate 287 — the highway empties into Routes 202 and 31 and Route 206. The DOT is now studying Route 206 — they found that traffic on Route 31 has increased from 700 to 3,000 trucks per day.

But DOT officials wrote to Kiser that a September 1994 inspection found that the bridges' condition had "stabilized" since 1992. They are still safe for 80,000-pound trucks, the letter said, "in spite of their deteriorated condition."

"THAT'S LIKE saying I checked the yogurt in my fridge a year ago and the date hadn't expired, so it's still good yogurt," said township Committeeman Carl Mayer. "I think that it is irrational not to do a new inspection, at a minimum, especially with the increases in truck traffic — and with an engineer requesting it like Bob Kiser."

Kiser was chosen as the 1994 Engineer of the Year by the New Jersey

● see BRIDGE, A10

'If something isn't done, the bridge will ultimately be structurally compromised to the point where it will have to be closed.'

— Dr. Winton Manning, traffic safety activist

The Times
TUESDAY, JUNE 20, 1995

Taxpayers can now digest budget 'pie charts'

By DAVID NEWHOUSE
Staff Writer

PRINCETON TOWNSHIP — The township committee last night voted to send out budget "pie charts" with this year's tax bills, but rejected a proposal by Committeeman Carl Mayer to furnish taxpayers with more information.

Township tax bills to be sent out next week will, for the first time, include charts — suggested by Mayer — showing the sources of revenue for this year's $19.3 million budget and the major areas of municipal spending.

But along with a "user-friendly" chart, Mayer had asked officials to include a five-year history of the tax rate, the budget total and the rate of inflation.

The motion to send the pie-chart data passed 4-1, but Mayer was so angered by the result of last night's debate that he cast the lone vote against what had, as far as it went, been his idea. He then left the meeting during a break that followed the vote.

Mayer had made including more information with tax bills a central issue in his campaign last fall, calling it a Taxpayer's Bill of Rights.

"I want to see the taxpayer provided with as much information as the shareholder in a company would have — because that's what they really are," Mayer said. But other committee members last night were skeptical about providing more data without looking carefully at how such data might be understood — especially the history of budget totals.

"Budgets are driven by all kinds of things," Committeeman Steven Frakt said, including state mandates and changes in the interest rate. "You talk about obfuscation — but if I've learned anything in two years up here, not to mention 25 years in Trenton, it's that you can get all kinds of people saying all kinds of things which are obfuscating. You can do as much harm as good pro-

viding information that can be misinterpreted."

Committee members said they had only received the proposed pie charts from township staff on April 27, and only heard recently that Mayer wanted more. Most committee members said they support the basic idea but felt it had been proposed too late.

Frakt volunteered to work on including more data in September's residents' newsletter. "It's just a matter of time, Carl," he said.

But Mayer, upset at the delay, said he had made the same proposal in January. "My proposals went far beyond this (pie chart)," he said. Besides the five-year trends, he had

suggested a chart showing how the township's tax rate stacks up to neighboring towns.

"It's very, very basic," Mayer insisted.

Assistant Administrator Susan Stanbury worried that too much information concerning the municipal tax rate — which is 21 percent of the total tax bill — might confuse taxpayers.

Committeewoman Phyllis Marchand added, "I think this (pie chart sheet) is good information for taxpayers. But I also, as a member of a 'corporation', would object to extra money being paid now for something which can be done another time."

"You want to get rid of the costs? Take it out of my salary," Mayer shot back. The extra copy work would cost just over $400, Administrator James Pascale said.

Part of the problem, Mayer had said earlier, comes from the fact that the state requires towns to keep their books in an obscure form. "It's like reading hieroglyphics," he said.

"You can pick up the annual report of a huge corporation like EXXON and, in a few minutes, find the essential information" to understand the company's financial picture, he said. "In Princeton Township, you can pick up 20 pages, reams of paper, and you have no clue."

237

Carl J. Mayer

CANDIDATES' FORUM

Township taxpayers deserve 'Bill of Rights'

To the editor:

I propose a Taxpayers Bill of Rights in Princeton Township. The first plank in this Bill of Rights is a readily understandable and user-friendly property tax bill.

As The Princeton Packet's editorial page has noted in the past, the annual bill presented to taxpayers in the township is hardly a model of clarity and lucid information. Indeed, if a bill were submitted to a customer in any other context, the customer would send the bill back to the vendor for insufficient information. Even local utility bills — prepared by large monopolies — give far more information than township tax bills. Ironically, for most taxpayers in the township, the largest check they will write during the course of the year — other than one to the IRS — will be their property tax bill.

Township property tax bills neglect a number of important variables. Have taxes risen faster than the rate of inflation? Can't tell. Where do

our taxes go, as a percentage basis, and with any degree of particularity? Can't tell. Are the budgets of the government entities that use our taxes — the school board, the Township Committee and county government — rising faster than the rate of inflation? Can't tell.

The first plank of a Princeton Township Taxpayers Bill of Rights should be to require that the annual property tax bill be user-friendly. In my opinion, it is the obligation of government to treat taxpayers as valued customers, not just automatic check-writers.

The new tax bill would give tables and charts that compare each taxpayers bill to the preceding five-year period. I propose that each bill have the following components: comparisons to the rate of inflation; comparisons to other municipal tax rates in this county; comparisons to the municipal tax rates with comparable socio-economic profiles in New Jersey. Finally, each bill should have contain a toll-free number that taxpayers can call to find out 1) how to appeal their property tax assessments; 2) how to readily obtain a clear copy of the township and other relevant budgets; and 3) how to obtain any further information.

This is the first plank in a Taxpayers Bill of Rights. It is based on conversations with tax-payers and homeowners I have met in the township while campaigning door to door. The appropriate slogan might be: "No taxation without clear presentation."

If taxpayers have other suggestions for how better to improve the tax bills or the tax system generally, please call. Other planks in the Bill of Rights will be discussed as the campaign unfolds. I hope these ideas will serve to improve public participation in the process, and allow our dedicated township officials to more effectively conduct township business.

Carl J. Mayer
58 Battle Road
Princeton Township

* * *

Candidates for municipal offices seeking election on Nov. 8 are encouraged to use this space to communicate their views.

238

THE NEW YORK TIMES, SUNDAY, MAY 29, 1994

PRACTICAL TRAVELER

A Non-Smoker Vs. an Airline

Stuart Goldberg

By BETSY WADE

A LAW professor who sued Air France in 1991 because he sat among smokers despite being assigned a nonsmoking seat won his breach-of-contract suit and was awarded $500 by the court, which the airline paid at the end of March.

The case, in the Small Claims part of New York City's Civil Court, does not constitute an overwhelming precedent; the judge says her decision was based on narrow grounds. But she followed her award with a written decision, an unusual step in Small Claims Court. And the plaintiff, Prof. Carl J. Mayer of the Hofstra University Law School on Long Island, and others on the antismoking ramparts believe the small claims forum provides an opening against foreign airlines whose overseas flights do not generally fall under United States smoking restrictions. They are sometimes deaf to the pleas of travelers unable to tolerate smoke.

Neighbors Light Up

Professor Mayer's saga began in a way familiar to many nonsmokers who fly abroad. On Aug. 1, 1990, he was returning to New York from Moscow through Paris on Air France Flight 079. He confirmed his reservation for a nonsmoking seat with an agent. At the gate, he again confirmed it and got a nonsmoking boarding pass for seat 34D. Before takeoff, his testimony said, he saw passengers around him in rows 33 and 35 smoking, and they resumed after takeoff. Passengers to his left in row 34 also started smoking. Professor Mayer complained, and the steward said that smokers and nonsmokers had been mixed because of a computer problem. Professor Mayer asked to be moved, but the flight was full and he remained in 34D.

He said he wrote the airline, seeking an apology and compensation, but got neither. On July 5, 1991, he filed a case in Small Claims Court, where no lawyer is needed, although Professor Mayer is a lawyer. He asked for the cost of the whole round-trip ticket to Moscow, $1,600; the court's upper limit is $2,000. His principal claim was breach of contract by Air France, which was represented by its own counsel and the New York law firm of Graham & James. The case was argued before Judge Louise Gruner Gans of the City Civil Court, who was on rotation to Small Claims.

Judge Gans decided in Professor Mayer's favor on March 31, 1992, awarding him $500, and issued her written opinion (S.C.N.Y. 7241/1991) on Dec. 22, 1993, taking the step, she said in an interview, because Professor Mayer had filed a brief and wanted to litigate the issue. The airline retained its right to appeal.

Judge Gans wrote that Air France's printed ticket disclaimer that it could not guarantee a nonsmoking seat was ambiguous and that Professor Mayer was thus entitled to rely on the word of employees and the notice on his boarding pass.

After the award was handed down but before the opinion was issued, Air France and Professor Mayer said, the airline offered him a $3,000 settlement, which he did not accept. Professor Mayer said he hoped the opin-

Continued ➔

ion would encourage others to use the small-claims route.

A spokesman for Air France said that it initially considered the case without merit. It filed a notice of appeal to keep its options open lest Judge Gans's opinion be far-reaching, but found it could live with the written opinion and withdrew its appeal on March 9.

Double Error

Walter J. Winnitzki of Manhasset, L.I., who is not a lawyer, got into a similar struggle with British Airways about his Oct. 1, 1993, flight to New York from London. Mr. Winnitzki, who recently had surgery for a collapsed lung, also could not resolve the seat problem during the flight. Initially given a smoking seat in error, he had it changed. An airline employee, then seeking a nonsmoking seat for another passenger, noted the original assignment, assumed that was acceptable to him and moved him to a smoking seat, from which he could not then be moved.

Mr. Winnitzki began a correspondence with the airline. He cited Department of Transportation rules saying that nonsmoking seats must be provided to those who request them (Code of Federal Regulations 252), and a reference to this rule printed on the ticket cover for his flight from New York, aboard American Airlines. He then learned, like others before him, that the smoking rules, other than those covering flights between two points in the United States, apply only to United States-certified airlines.

Smoking is banned by Regulation 252 on flights of six hours or less between two points both in the United States, Puerto Rico and the Virgin Islands, and this includes flights of six hours or less going to or from Alaska or Hawaii or linking Alaska and Hawaii. The rule applies to foreign as well as domestic lines flying such a route.

On direct flights outside the United States, domestic airlines are required by Regulation 252 to provide nonsmoking seats in each class to every passenger who wants one who holds a reservation and meets the check-in deadline for the flight. Further, the rule says that if a nonsmoking section is between two smoking sections, the passengers in the middle are not to be "unreasonably burdened."

Tightening the Rules

John F. Banzhaf 3d, executive director of the private antismoking group, Action on Smoking and Health, first sought nonsmoking sections in airplanes in 1969, and, as pressure mounted, they were created in 1973, the top of a 21-year slippery slope so far as smokers are concerned. Professor Banzhaf, who teaches law at the George Washington University Law Center in Washington, worries a lot these days about the problems of nonsmokers on foreign airlines.

At Aviation Subcommittee hearings on Airliner Cabin Air Quality in Congress on May 18, Professor Banzhaf submitted a proposal for an emergency regulation to forbid seating children in smoking sections, citing their vulnerability to environmental tobacco smoke. "We keep children out of casinos and bars," Professor Banzhaf said, "even though no tangible harm results and they may not be aware of their surroundings."

His second proposal is that the United States take steps toward fulfilling the United Nations resolution that smoking be banned on all flights by July 1, 1996. He suggested that the Government enter into agreements with Canada and Mexico covering flights linking the United States and their countries.

The Aviation Subcommittee, for its part, was preparing legislation to ban smoking on all international flights by United States lines. Caroline Gabel, a professional staff member for the subcommittee, said the bill should have been filed by this weekend.

Action on Smoking and Health, known as ASH, has prepared a letter to be handed to flight attendants and other airline employees in the event of conflict over seating, outlining the rules governing United States airline flights. This focuses on the "unreasonably burdened" provision — for instance, that the drifting smoke might activate an allergy — and a requirement to expand a nonsmoking section if need be. The back of the letter contains a warning about possible complaints and fines and the text of the rules. A copy is available to those sending a stamped self-addressed envelope to Smoking Letter, ASH, 2013 H Street, N.W., Washington, D.C. 20006. ∎

BY RAYMOND E. JUNGWIRTH, C.S.C.S.

Future Trends In Personal Training

Today your clients are exposed to more information about fitness than ever before. As a personal trainer, you must also be an educator.

To continue serving your well informed market, you must stay current with the latest information and trends. A strong education and experience in the field is your best bet. Combining education with your gym experience will help you become a successful trainer. A college degree or certification from a professional organization is an ideal way to confirm you possess a certain level of knowledge.

When you are ready to tackle the world of personal training, you should keep in mind personal training is a luxury item and often the first appointment scratched from a client's busy schedule, making your role as a trainer even more important. Your business depends on getting clients to commit and be responsible for their own fitness. To accomplish this give them unconditional attention, even to the smallest detail, during their training sessions. Offer a time efficient work out and structure a fitness program to meet their goals and schedules.

There are definite advantages to working in a health club—no overhead costs, a captive market and no driving time in between appointments. The drawback may be you have to work for the club, pay a percentage to the club or both. If you work in your client's home you can charge more, but will have operating costs such as vehicle main-tenance and equipment. Owning your own studio can be rewarding, however you also assume the risk and expenses.

One of the best ways to market yourself is by doing a good job every time you step on to the floor. Others in the room will notice this and approach you, and your name will come up every time your client's friends notice their improved appearance. Remember, to do your best job you must put a new smile on every hour. You are somebody different to each client—

Your job does not end at simply being a personal trainer.

Ray Jungwirth, athletic director at Club Sport of Pleasanton, California.

friend, counselor, motivator, etc. So know when to push and when to pull.

Run your business like any other business. Have every client sign an agreement which clearly states your policies regarding rescheduling, cancellations and no shows. Let your clients know the work they do with you is only part of their entire fitness program. They need to eat right, get adequate rest and reduce stress. Besides your technical abilities, the key to being a good personal trainer is to be a good communicator. Attempt to achieve a flawless set of customer service skills and adapt to the many different types of client personalities. Always maintain a professional attitude and appearance and use a practical application of all your technical skills.

The market is good for those who are willing to be flexible and continue to pursue excellence, but the future is now. Don't wait until tomorrow to start your own personal development, you can bet your competition isn't waiting! **AF**

Ray Jungwirth is the athletic director at Club Sport of Pleasanton, California.

Can't Afford A Private Trainer? Try A Public Workout

The energy Americans currently expend on exercise could be transformed into one of our greatest national resources. Instead of emphasizing individual achievement, Americans could compete athletically to improve public life. The replacement of private workouts with "public workouts" would invigorate the body and spirit of American communities.

Americans spend millions of hours every year jogging, biking, swimming, weightlifting and engaging in virtually every sport imaginable. The motion and energy currently devoted to solitary exercise could easily be redirected to improve America's neighborhoods. Bicyclists could pick up and deliver packages and groceries for the elderly. Joggers could run through parks cleaning up litter or assist police patrols. Weightlifters could supplement their workout in the gym with lifting brick and mortar for community centers or housing for the homeless.

These "public workouts" would provide the athlete with the same amount of physical training they are accustomed and in the process neighborhoods across the country would receive tangible dividends. In high crime neighborhoods in cities like New York, joggers and bikers could supplement police forces that badly need to increase the presence of law and order on the streets. Individualistic, competitive training techniques could be transformed into community-centered, participatory methods. This would not only provide energy and inspiration for our neighborhoods, it would break the monotony for the athlete in his or her weekly training regimen.

No one is suggesting America's amateur athletes be required to perform community service. But the opportunity to do so should be made available on a daily basis. Each community could identify the needs of people that could be met using the pre-existing motion of exercise. Those who take their daily exercise in this fashion would receive the additional benefit of meeting other like-minded individuals.

Such a coordinated system of "public workouts" would have several advantages over special events. The solution to a particular problem, for example, often requires more than simply throwing money at it. The involvement of neighbors and athletes in a common problem would invigorate community spirit.

A common American trait is a restlessness and energy frequently manifested in exercise. If only a fraction of this enthusiasm were diverted regularly to community projects, the public life of the country would be greatly enriched.

The day may arrive when the amateur athlete in America speaks not just of their "personal best," but also their community best.

—Carl J. Mayer

Carl J. Mayer

Foreigners are ripping off our resources

Denver Post Trail E

CARL J. MAYER

ALTHOUGH Americans just fought a war to secure petroleum resources halfway around the globe, we're giving away precious mineral resources at home. In the last few years, foreign multinational companies have acquired, for virtually nothing, the nation's most valuable gold deposits. In extracting this bounty, these same foreign conglomerates are ruining the environment of America's most pristine land.

All this is being accomplished under an arcane 19th century law that permits mining on public lands — property collectively owned by all Americans and managed by the federal government. Over 732 million acres of public lands (a fourth of the country) is open to mining.

Incredibly, the law — the 1872 Mining Act — still permits anyone to enter public lands and take valuable minerals free, including gold, silver and copper. The land can be bought outright for as little as $2.50 an acre, about the price of popcorn in a movie theater.

Foreign corporations are exploiting this outdated provision to extract billions of dollars of gold and other minerals from public lands located primarily in the Western states: California, Colorado, Nevada, Oregon, Utah and Wyoming.

This giveaway is so astonishing because these gold resources are owned by you and me: the taxpayer. If the Rockefeller family sells Rockefeller Center to Mitsubishi bank, that may be their business. But if the American government donates the nation's valuable mineral deposits — resources held in trust for all the people — to foreign firms, this is decidedly a matter for the American citizenry.

Consider some recent exploits of foreign multinationals:

✔ Newmont Mining Corp. — owned jointly by British and Australians — has opened a gargantuan gold mine on public land in Nevada. This quarry reaches down into the earth the length of a football field; colossal dump trucks cart 200,000-pound loads of gold-bearing rock. While this mine is slated to yield reserves worth $6 billion at current prices, the citizen-owners of this property will receive nothing in return.

✔ Sometimes foreign corporations brazenly speculate with U.S. property. Recently, the government sold 17,000 acres of public mineral land to an unidentified foreign speculator for $42,500; weeks later, the new owners peddled this same land to the British-owned Shell Oil Co. for $34 million. (Shell admits it has no plans to actually mine the land.)

✔ Canadian corporations, like Echo Bay Mines Co. and American Barrack Resources Co., have been gobbling up public acreage. Typical is a large-scale gold mine planned by Noranda Minerals Co. of Canada near Cooke City, Mont. The proposed mine site is within 2 miles of Yellowstone Park and the Absarokee-Beartooth Wilderness. Already, exposed rock at the mine site is leaching poisonous drainage into two adjacent streams, both of which feed into tributaries of the Yellowstone River.

Although modern mining methods pollute streams and scar landscapes, the ancient 1872 Mining Law has no provisions for protecting public land. Nothing prevents foreign corporations from deserting mine sites and leaving behind waste piles, dangerous pits and caustic chemicals like sulfuric acid and cyanide. The mining industry generates twice as much solid waste annually as that carted to industrial and municipal landfills combined; abandoned mines are fast becoming the Superfund sites of the future.

Despite this, the Interior Department remains uninterested in ever identifying foreign operators on our public lands. Although the Agriculture Department annually publishes a list of foreign owners of U.S. agricultural land, nothing comparable exists for much more valuable mineral land. If a foreigner owns a clump of United States dirt, he has to report it to the world; if the same foreigner acquires our gold, nobody is the wiser. For all we know, foreigners control every dime of public mineral production in America.

There is no reason to xenophobically reject all foreign activity on public lands, but Americans are at least entitled to know whether there is reciprocity. Can American corporations mine free on foreign-owned lands?

Most countries, like Australia and Canada, carefully monitor foreign mining. And every other country in the world assesses some royalty on mineral production; applied here, this would result annually in hundreds of millions of dollars of federal revenue.

Considering that opinion surveys indicate that three-quarters of Americans fear U.S. sovereignty is threatened by foreign investment (which now totals $2 trillion), we should at least know the extent that other nations determine our mineral destiny. Americans were loathe to permit the Yellowstone Park concession to fall into the hands of Matsushita, a Japanese company. And Congress has banned the export of timber, taken from federal lands, to Japan.

Now is the time to plan the fate of our most valuable public mineral resources.

Recently Arkansas Sen. Dale Bumpers and West Virginia Congressman Nick Rahall introduced legislation to repeal the 1872 Mining Law. This would at least loosen the grip of foreign interests on American mineral land.

Write to your congressman to support this effort.

Carl J. Mayer, an assistant professor at Hofstra Law School, testified last fall before the U.S. Congress Subcommittee on Mining and Natural Resources

Denver Post
4/6/91

242

Corporate Lobby Muffled —And It's About Time, Too

By Carl J. Mayer

IN THEIR most recent First Amendment opinion, the nine Supreme Court justices did more to advance the cause of campaign finance reform than any politician probably ever will.

The justices upheld the right of one state, Michigan, to prohibit corporations from financially backing political candidates. This landmark opinion paves the way for other states to reduce the corrosive influence of money on politics.

Here is how the case arose. In the mid-1970s, Michigan passed a campaign-finance law that forbade corporations from using general treasury funds — owned by shareholders but controlled by management — to make independent expenditures in a political campaign. This meant, for instance, that corporations could no longer advertise or print leaflets on a candidate's behalf.

In 1985, the Michigan Chamber of Commerce, in an attempt to challenge the law, decided to spend money to support a candidate for the state house of representatives. The chamber, an organization comprised of Michigan's most powerful corporate interests, backed the candidate most amenable to the chamber's pro-

Carl J. Mayer teaches law at Hofstra Law School. His works include a recent law review article on corporations and the Bill of Rights.

business agenda: primarily, the reduction of workers' compensation benefits.

A federal district court judge found that the chamber's activities breached Michigan's campaign finance law. The chamber appealed, and the Sixth Circuit Court of Appeals reversed, holding that the finance law violated the First Amendment rights of the chamber. (This argument relied on a precedent holding that certain restrictions on spending amount to an impingement on free speech.)

Only a few days ago the Supreme Court reversed again by a 6-3 margin, setting a weighty precedent. The court's powerful opinion, written by Justice Thurgood Marshall, distinguished between individual speech and corporate speech in the form of cash doled out to politicians. While individual speech remains largely inviolate, a corporation's spending can be curbed to prevent, in the court's words, the "serious

> 'The court safeguarded the rights of minority shareholders.'

danger [that] corporate political expenditures will undermine the integrity of the political process."

This Supreme Court opinion ends the ability of corporate interests to hide behind the First Amendment to justify lavish campaign contributions. The court wisely reasoned that because the state accords corporations valuable benefits (like limited liability and favorable tax treatment), the state can exercise a greater control over corporations than over individuals. "These state-created advantages not only allow corporations to play a dominant role in the nation's economy," ruled the court, "but also permit them to use resources amassed in the economic marketplace to obtain an unfair advantage in the political marketplace."

The court's opinion did nothing to diminish the First Amendment rights of individuals. Officers, directors, or other members of a corporation remain free, of course, to contribute to political campaigns. But by restricting corporate speech, the court safeguarded the rights of minority shareholders who do not hold the same views as those advanced on the corporation's behalf by senior managers.

In the past, top corporate officers have used the corporation as a personal mouthpiece, doling out corporate dollars to political cronies or to pet causes. This abuse of the corporate entity not only wasted shareholder money, but also forced dissenting shareholders to associate with speech they opposed. No more.

The most heartening aspect of the Supreme Court's recent opinion is that archliberal Thurgood Marshall and archconservative William Rehnquist joined forces for the majority. The agreement of ideological antagonists reflects the screaming need to counteract the cash corruption of American politics. In one intrepid opinion, a convincing Supreme Court majority has emboldened reformers and provided politicians with the tools for change.

Perhaps other states will follow Michigan's example and silence, or at least mute, the corporate lobby. The nation cannot afford many more $500 billion scandals such as the one involving the savings and loan industry, which wasted depositor money on cash contributions to elected officials.

Whatever the outcome of reform, the court has appropriately ruled, during the bicentennial of the Bill of Rights, that the First Amendment should protect individuals, not license corporate payoffs to politicians.

NEWSDAY, THURSDAY, MAY 3, 1990

243

THE NEW YORK TIMES, SATURDAY, APRIL 9, 1988

Corporations Are Not Persons

By Ralph Nader and Carl J. Mayer

WASHINGTON

Our constitutional rights were intended for real persons, not artificial creations. The Framers certainly knew about corporations but chose not to mention these contrived entities in the Constitution. For them, the document shielded *living* beings from arbitrary government and endowed them with the right to speak, assemble and petition.

Today, however, corporations enjoy virtually the same umbrella of constitutional protections as individuals do. They have become in effect artificial persons with infinitely greater power than humans. This constitutional equivalence must end.

Consider a few noxious developments during the last 10 years. A group of large Boston companies invoked the First Amendment in order to spend lavishly and thus successfully defeat a referendum that would have permitted the legislature to enact a progressive income tax that had no direct effect on the property and business of these companies. An

Ralph Nader, a consumer advocate, directs the Corporate Accountability Research Group. Carl J. Mayer is a graduate student in law at Harvard Law School.

Idaho electrical and plumbing corporation cited the Fourth Amendment and deterred a health and safety investigation. A textile supply company used Fifth Amendment protections and barred retrial in a criminal antitrust case in Texas.

The idea that the Constitution should apply to corporations as it applies to humans had its dubious origins in 1886. The Supreme Court said it did "not wish to hear argument" on whether corporations were "persons" protected by the 14th Amendment, a civil rights amendment designed to safeguard newly emancipated blacks from unfair government treatment. It simply decreed that corporations were persons.

Now *that* is judicial activism. A string of later dissents, by Justices Hugo Black and William O. Douglas, demonstrated that neither the history nor the language of the 14th Amendment was meant to protect corporations. But it was too late. The genie was out of the bottle and the corporate evolution into personhood was under way.

It was not until the 1970's that corporations began to throw their constitutional weight around. Recent court decisions suggest that the future may hold even more dramatic extensions of corporate protections.

In 1986, Dow Chemical, arguing before the Supreme Court, suggested that the Fourth Amendment's prohibition against unreasonable searches and seizures should prohibit the Environmental Protection Agency from flying planes over Dow's manufacturing facilities to monitor compliance with environmental laws. Although the Court permitted the flights on technical grounds, it appeared to endorse Dow's expansive view of the Constitution.

That year, corporations received the most sweeping enlargement of their free speech rights to date. In a 5-3 decision, the Court invalidated a California regulation ordering a public utility monopoly to enclose in its billing envelopes a communication

This legal equivalence must end.

from a nonprofit rate-payer advocacy group that financed the insert. The purpose of the regulation was to assist the Public Utility Commission in achieving its authorized goal of reasonable rates. Even so, the Court held that the enclosures violated a new corporate First Amendment right "not to speak." Associate Justice William H. Rehnquist wrote in a pro-consumer dissent that to "ascribe to such artificial entities an 'intellect' or 'mind' [for constitutional purposes] is to confuse metaphor with reality."

Today, corporations remain unsatisfied with their ascendant constitu-

Continued →

tional status. They want much more. At a 1987 judicial conference in Pennsylvania, lawyers counseled that corporations use the First Amendment to invalidate a range of Federal regulations, including Securities and Exchange Commission disclosure requirements that govern corporate takeovers, and rules affecting stock offerings.

Businesses angry at Congressional attempts to ban cigarette advertising — by that, we mean commercial carcinogenic speech — are alleging First Amendment violations.

The corporate drive for constitutional parity with real humans comes at a time when legislatures are awarding these artificial persons superhuman privileges. Besides perpetual life, corporations enjoy limited liability for industrial accidents such as nuclear power disasters, and the use of voluntary bankruptcy and other disappearing acts to dodge financial obligations while remaining in business.

The legal system is thus creating unaccountable Frankensteins that have human powers but are nonetheless constitutionally shielded from much actual and potential law enforcement as well as from accountability to real persons such as workers, consumers and taxpayers.

Of course individuals in these companies can always exercise their personal constitutional rights, but the drive for corporate rights is dangerously out of control.

Too frequently the extension of corporate constitutional rights is a zero-sum game that diminishes the rights and powers of real individuals. The corporate exercise of First Amendment rights frustrates the individual's right to participate more equally in democratic elections, to pay reasonable utility rates and to live in a toxin-free environment. Fourth Amendment rights applied to the corporation diminish the individual's right to live in an unpolluted world and to enjoy privacy.

Equality of constitutional rights plus an inequality of legislated and de facto powers leads inevitably to the supremacy of artificial over real persons. And now the ultimate irony: Corporate entities have the constitutional right, says the Supreme Court, to patent living beings such as genetically engineered cattle, pigs, chickens and, perhaps someday, humanoids.

This is not to say that corporations should have only the legal rights emanating from state charters that create them. What is required, however, is a constitutional presumption favoring the individual over the corporation.

To establish this presumption, we need a constitutional amendment that declares that corporations are not persons and that they are only entitled to statutory protections conferred by legislatures and through referendums. Only then will the Constitution become the exclusive preserve of those whom the Framers sought to protect: real people.   □

Carl J. Mayer

Reverse Reagan's Ruinous Federal Land-Sale Policies

By Carl J. Mayer

IN THE WANING days of the Reagan administration, the Interior Department took measures to accelerate the transfer of America's public lands to private developers. This land grab confirmed, sadly, that privatization and speculation superseded environmental and public-interest concerns during the Reagan years. The Bush administration must act decisively to protect America's fragile public domain; failure to do so will further distance the Republican Party from its noble, if battered, conservationist heritage.

Ronald Reagan's most alarming 11th-hour move was the promise to immediately begin transferring thousands of acres of federal oil shale land, predominantly in Colorado — potentially some of the most valuable real estate in the world — to private speculators for $2.50 per acre. (Oil shale is a mineral that can be converted into petroleum at very high temperatures. If the conversion process is ever perfected, scientists believe that public oil shale lands could yield 50 percent more than all of OPEC's known reserves.)

Production of oil from shale, however, is not now commercially feasible. After having wasted millions of taxpayer dollars on mismanaged oil shale and other synthetic fuel projects, now is not the time for the government to provide land, virtually free, to a moribund industry. The only beneficiaries will be speculators who, in recent years, have already purchased public oil shale land for $2.50 per acre and immediately resold these same lands for more than $2,000 per acre. Worse still, once this land passes out of federal control, environmental regulation becomes nearly impossible.

As if the oil shale grab was not sufficiently profligate, the Reagan administration also proposed lowering the royalties that corporations pay for coal mined on public lands. This coal is owned by all Americans, and the government has a constitutional obligation to

'Bush must return to the historic values of Republican conservationism.'

manage it responsibly. But the Interior Department prepared rules during Reagan's last days that would lower the royalty rate for certain federal coal from 8 percent to 5 percent of the gross sale price. The United States already charges lower royalties for government-owned minerals than almost any other country, including many Third World nations. (Royalties from minerals leased on federal lands are the government's second largest source of revenue after income taxes; critics contend that these revenues would be much higher if the government assessed the 15 percent or 20 percent charged by many other nations.)

While lowering coal royalties, the Reagan Interior Department also proposed regulations that would permit corporations to mine in national parks. Environmentalists contend that under these rules areas like the New River Gorge National Park in West Virginia would be endangered. Even worse, on his final day in office, Reagan's interior secretary, Donald Hodel, proposed drilling for oil and gas in parts of the Arctic National Wildlife Refuge — a breeding ground for herds of migrating caribou.

In aggregate, these maneuvers pose a dangerous threat to the nation's rapidly dwindling public lands and mark the historic low point in the Republican rejection of environmentalism at the Interior Department.

The Republican Party did not always advocate such foolhardy public land policies. At the turn of the century, Teddy Roosevelt led the party's conservationist Bull Moose wing, and helped create our National Park System.

Since the Progressive era, however, Republican environmentalism has steadily declined. Irresponsible Republican Interior Department practices really began in the 1920s with the Teapot Dome scandal, when Interior Secretary Albert Fall became the first Cabinet member to serve time in jail after having traded public land leases to two oil tycoons for cash bribes. The Reagan years brought us James Watt and an Interior Department willing to permit mining adjacent to the crown jewels of Teddy Roosevelt's cherished national parks: Glacier, Yellowstone and the Grand Canyon. The last-minute moves by Reagan's Interior Department appeared to signal a final turn away from environmentalism.

If candidate George Bush meant what he said about the importance of the environment, President Bush

Carl J. Mayer is the Golieb Fellow in Legal History at New York University's School of Law. He has written widely on public land issues.

Continued →

SECOND OPINION

Van Howell

must return to the historic values of Republican conservationism and undo Reagan's last-minute assault on public lands.

Three steps are necessary. First, the Interior Department must stop giving away oil shale claims for $2.50 an acre. If it doesn't, Congress should declare a moratorium on such sales. Second, Interior should rescind rules that would lower the royalties paid to the public Treasury and instead, consider raising the rates. Finally, the president should make it clear that no mining or drilling will ever take place in the national park system created by his Republican ancestor.

Bush's interior secretary, Manuel Lujan Jr., has not made a promising start. Almost immediately after his swearing in, Lujan embarked on a 10-day junket to sunny Guam, Hawaii, Samoa and other Pacific Trust Islands. Before going, Lujan failed to appoint any assistant secretaries, leaving the department to languish. Now, having just returned, the secretary must face up to the grave threats to America's most precious natural heritage.

NEWSDAY, THURSDAY, MARCH 2, 1989

ABOUT THE AUTHOR

Carl J. Mayer is an attorney, author, elected official, and consumer advocate. He was the first Independent elected in Princeton, New Jersey. He has been featured on the CBS news program "Sixty Minutes" and has published articles in the *New York Times*, *Newsday*, *The Newark-Star Ledger*, *The Asbury Park Press* and in many other papers and journals. A former law professor and assistant to Ralph Nader, Carl Mayer clerked for United States District Court Judge Caleb M. Wright. He is a graduate of Princeton University (magna cum laude), Chicago Law School and Harvard Law School.